Scotland
REDISCOVERED

Scotland
REDISCOVERED

Photographs by
DENNIS HARDLEY

Text by Sir Harry Boyne

B.T. BATSFORD LTD · LONDON

ISBN 0 7134 5126 2

Printed in Hong Kong
for the publisher
B.T. Batsford Ltd
4 Fitzhardinge Street London W1H 0AH

HALF-TITLE PAGE

M cCaig's Tower (or 'Folly')
dominates a yachtsman's
landfall view of the handsome
Argyllshire town of Oban among
its tree-clad hills. It is nearly 100
years since McCaig, a philanthropic
banker, built this unfinished replica
of the Parthenon to provide jobs for
local craftsmen and also serve as a
family memorial. Its walls, two feet
thick, stand 30-47 feet high. An
observation platform on the seaward
side is a recent addition.

TITLE PAGE

T he rugged scenery around
Inchnadamph, viewed from
Ardvreck Castle, a mile or so above
the town. The castle, built in 1597
to serve as seat for the McLeods of
Assynt, was the site of The Marquess
of Montrose's betrayal for £20,000 in
1650. Montrose was led to Edinburgh
and hanged on 21 May—said to be
the only occasion when one
Highlander betrayed another in
war for financial gain.

The photographs

Grandiose, mainly Victorian buildings surround Glasgow's George Square—a colourful sight in spring time. Also known as 'Glasgow's Valhalla', it contains monuments to Sir Walter Scott and James Watt as well as a War Memorial. The square was laid out in 1781, and is named after King George III.

The graceful grassy heights of the
Eildon Hills, a few miles from
Melrose with its lovely Abbey,
convey to perfection the essentially
placid beauty of 'the Borders'. Yet
evidence of towers, keeps and castles
abounds to remind us that this land
of peace and plenty was for centuries
the scene of ruthless bloody warfare
between Scots and English.

Libraries and family bookshelves all over the world are seldom without books about Scotland. They have poured from the presses for 150 years or more—certainly since Sir Walter Scott romanticized his native land and Queen Victoria fell in love with it. The inspiration behind this book is the photography of Dennis Hardley, who has spent 14 years travelling throughout Scotland, seeking views of town and country perhaps unfamiliar to many readers. Even the few widely known subjects in the book are seen all the more vividly with the eyes of one of our greatest landscape photographers. An Englishman who chose an entirely new life-style in Scotland, he is unprejudiced as well as percipient. His field of artistic vision is unconfined by partiality for any particular region of the infinitely picturesque and varied country he has come to cherish as his own. So a native Scot may have to turn these pages in vain for the familiar, more hackneyed view. Or, if he does come across a Hardley study of a favourite subject, he may not at first glance recognise it. Hence 'Scotland Rediscovered'. The fresh eye of a photo-artist from Cheshire, allied with the insight and patience necessary to capture the perfect conjunction of light, shade and colour, will reveal new aspects of the familiar as well as unfolding for lifelong devotees of Scottish scenery a wealth of recondite charms which they will yearn to see for themselves.

The writer's role in this venture is merely as accompanist to the virtuoso. I'm a Scotsman, it is true, indeed a Highlander, born in Inverness before the First World War. But I made my home in the London area 36 years ago, although I have been a frequent visitor to many parts of Scotland ever since. My first 40 years were spent in Inverness, in Dundee, in a Highland regiment, in Dundee again and in Edinburgh. My long residence in central and suburban London since then may have qualified me to see my native country more clearly in the perspective of the United Kingdom of which Scotland remains a respected and indispensable component. I have also had the advantage, as a political journalist, of being kept closely and constantly in touch with the administration of Scotland in all its aspects.

I wonder, for instance, how many of my coeval compatriots could claim to have known personally every Secretary of State for Scotland since Willie Adamson held that office in 1929-30, and to have been a confidant of most of them regardless of party. This experience enabled me to acquire inside knowledge from outside, as it were, of Scotland's economy as it has developed since the lean and hungry years which followed, for Britain as a whole, the defeat of Nazi Germany.

Mistakes have been made and opportunities missed, of course. But I

Morris's garden is but one among the many attractions of Abbotsford House, which Sir Walter Scott built for himself on Tweedside and where he died in 1832. It still contains his fascinatingly varied collection of memorabilia, armour, books and furniture.

should be surprised if any impartial observer who has lived in Scotland throughout those four decades would deny that the standard of living of the Scottish people in general has improved to a level which few could have contemplated in 1945. If politicians of successive Labour and Conservative administrations are to be given any credit at all for the improvement, some should also be spared for the Scottish National Party, if only because from time to time it deflated any tendency to complacency on the part of the others.

One thing which hasn't improved, I'll be told, is the Scottish weather. My answer is that it was never in any need of improvement. Scotland is a big country, about 60 per cent as large as England, and the prevailing weather varies, just as it does in England, from area to area. Thanks to the meteoroligical graphics we all see nowadays on television, the English assumption that everywhere north of the Border is cold and wet gains less credence than it did; but it is still apt to surface when family holiday plans are being debated.

The facts are that Scotland's annual rainfall can vary from less than 30 inches on the east coast to something not far short of 200 inches on the mountainous heights of Argyllshire, western Inverness-shire and Wester Ross. However, the effects of the superabundant 'precipitation' in those areas are not without their visual attraction, as may be judged from Hardley's winter view towards Aonach Dubh from the torrent-swollen River Coe (p. **16**). Latitude dictates that temperatures in Scotland are generally a few degrees lower than in the rest of Britain, but summers on the eastern side of the country, contrary to what one might expect, tend to be warmer as well as drier than on the west.

Coupled with the fact that summer daylight lasts longer the farther north you go, this perhaps accounts for my happy memories of wandering carefree round the midnight streets of Inverness or Dundee with other young reporters in June and July, blest with a climate that seems in recollection to have been as mild and balmy as Malaga's. As old soldiers who have route-marched in Scotland will readily confirm, a summer's afternoon can even get unbearably hot. There was obviously no lack of warm sunshine when Hardley came upon his charmingly tranquil version of Glen Etive, even though traces of winter snow on the Glencoe Hills were still to be seen (p. **17**).

The waters of this picturesque glen in Appin, Argyllshire, are in part derived from Rannoch Moor and reach the sea by way of Loch Etive. On the north shore of the loch are the ruins of the thirteenth-century Ardchattan Priory, notable for the conversion of the priors' demesne into a formal garden of shrubs, supplemented by herbaceous borders, roses and a wild garden. The gardens are open to visitors except in winter. As the arboreal study on page 18 suggests, they are probably at their best in the late summer—another 'plus' for September. For anecdotal evidence of the intense midsummer heat that may sometimes prevail in Appin we can turn to David Balfour's account in R. L. Stevenson's enthralling novel *Kidnapped*, of the long day he and Alan Breck spent hiding from the English redcoats in a shallow cleft between lofty rocks:

You are to remember that we lay on the bare top of a rock, like scones upon a girdle; the sun beat upon us cruelly; the rock grew so heated, a man could

Viewed from Pulpit Hill, little Kerrera and spacious Mull are among many Inner Hebridean islands easily accessible by ferry from Oban. This makes the town an ideal base from which to sample the restful charm of island life.

This evening view of Elie from the pier brings out the picturesque quality of the little maritime burghs strung along the coastline of the East Neuk (corner) of Fife. Elie and its close neighbour Earlsferry, overlooking the Firth of Forth, are noted for safe sandy beaches and also for having nurtured the greatest golfer of his time, James Braid.

15

The River Coe, from which this wintry study looks towards Aonach Dubh, is less familiar than the notorious glen, scene of the 1692 massacre, to which it gives its name. Glencoe is reckoned Scotland's most impressive glen, an awesome gorge stretching from Rannoch Moor to Loch Leven.

Glen Etive, from which this study directs one's gaze north towards the heights guarding Glencoe, descends with its river from Rannoch Moor and winds down to the point near Glenetive House where the Etive flows into the long sea loch of the same name. The legendary Deirdre of the Sorrows was reputedly exiled somewhere in Glen Etive.

scarce endure the touch of it; and the little patch of earth and fern, which keep cooler, was only large enough for one at a time. We took turn about to lie on the naked rock, which was indeed like the position of that saint that was martyred on a gridiron; and it ran in my mind how strange it was, that in the same climate and at only a few days' distance, I should have suffered so cruelly, first from cold upon my island and now from heat upon this rock.

That last reflection of David's neatly sums up the vagaries of Scotland's weather, which are not, however, without parallel elsewhere in the United Kingdom. I remember bales of hay being dropped by the Royal Air Force to succour cattle and sheep snowbound in the glens of Angus in June; but I also remember shivering with all London in the bitterly cold downpour of Coronation Day, 2 June 1953. The difference is that in Scotland your host will always have a blazing fire ready—and a stiff dram. *Vive la différence.*

Scotsmen are often asked to recommend the 'best' time of year to visit their country. I usually preface my reply with a reminder that every time of year, in every country, has its merits and its drawbacks; therefore the best is entirely a matter of personal choice. That said, my own preference is clear: June or September, with the later month just qualifying for the gold medal. In a 'normal' year, both months generally provide the attraction of moderate rainfall and ample sunshine. And they share the fascinating benefit of the long twilight with which, almost regardless of the prevailing weather, the Scottish summer is always blest.

What turns my personal scale against June, apart from the slight risk that it can sometimes be oppressively hot, is the fact that the daylight in mid-summer goes on too long for me. I have reached the age at which I'd rather sleep at midnight than roam in the gloaming, as Harry Lauder used to sing, 'wi' a lassie by my side'. Lauder is a name one seldom hears today, but in his time he was as effective an ambassador for Scotland as Walter Scott himself. In September the days are still quite long enough, the climate is agreeably mild with plenty of sunshine, and the entire countryside, in a spectrum varying from green to gold, looks enchanting.

Then there is the bonus of glorious sunsets which, though they can be very fine in Scotland at any time of year, are surely at their most ravishing in the early autumn. Dennis Hardley has wisely given us some examples, such as the view over Gourock and Clyde water from Lyle Hill (pp. **110-11**); the afterglow in Oban Bay (pp. **40-41**); the fading day mirrored in Loch Awe (pp. **126-27**); and the silhouette of the ruined cathedral to which St Andrews owes its name.

I think the English upper classes—the 'toffs' or the 'gentry' as we used to call them during my Inverness boyhood—knew what they were about when they came to their shooting lodges for 'the Twelfth' (of August) and remained through September. This is not only open season for killing grouse and other game but the sweet of the year in Scotland: the air as refreshing as the bouquet from a balloon of old cognac and so clear that the skyline recedes to infinity; the sheep-cropped grass springy under one's feet; the great expanses of flowering heather on moorland making a

The gardens and ruins of the thirteenth-century Ardchattan Priory, which was partly converted into a private residence some 350 years after its foundation, are on the north shore of Loch Etive, easily accessible by road from the loch-end at Ledaig, Argyllshire. Shrubs and flowers are probably the main attraction, but there are also some interesting carved stones and monuments.

19

The parish church at Dalmally, a village on the River Orchy, Argyllshire, looks entrancing in its freshly donned winter garb—though the new snowfall may have created problems for intending worshippers from farther up Glen Orchy.

OVERLEAF
When one looks at this autumnal view of the Pap of Glencoe, with its adjacent conical summits, it is not too difficult to surmise that the derivation of the name may bear some relation to the female anatomy.

20

veritable sight to dream about in the winter ahead. Dennis Hardley has captured more than a hint of those autumnal enticements in his views of the Pap of Glencoe (pp. **22-23**) and a placid lochan, or small lake, among the hills in much the same area of Argyll. No wonder all three generations of our present Royal Family, true to Queen Victoria's example, make autumn in Scotland their favourite holiday season. We occasionally ate grouse at home—my father, a local journalist on good terms with the lairds, was in the way of receiving presents of game, salmon, hares and so on, and my mother, a gamekeeper's daughter, certainly knew how to cook them. But I can't say I found grouse a gourmet's delight worth the price they fetch in West End restaurants.

I never fired, let alone possessed, a shotgun. However, for a season or two I was a casual beater on an estate in Strathnairn where a wealthy Clyde shipbuilder had the shooting. It was a perfect day out for an active youngster. Nothing to do but drive the birds over the butts with shouts and waving arms, and then enjoy an *al fresco* lunch of roast beef sandwiches and lemonade (the men got bottled beer). Meanwhile we viewed with fascination and not the slightest resentment the guns and their tweed-clad ladies sit down to a sumptuous meal served on a snow-white tablecloth with all the panoply of silver, china and crystal brought from the 'Big House'.

Best of all, of course, was the payment—from memory, about 7s 6d (37p) a day. I thought it very generous, as indeed it was in the 1920s. An added advantage was that the factor (estate agent) wisely withheld his accounting until December, when a postal order would arrive in good time for the festive season.

The appeal of grouse shooting seems to be more widespread than ever nowadays, with oil-rich Arab sheikhs and princelings vying with American financiers and Continental captains of industry to rent sought-after moors. Syndicates of English (and Scottish) businessmen are also in the market, with each member willing to subscribe as much as he can afford for the chance of a day or two out with his shotgun.

Apparently the reason why heather-clad moors on high ground are the habitat of the red grouse is that the bird relies on young heather shoots for most of its nourishment and on long heather for sheltered nesting. So grouse and heather complement each other. It is important for the Highland economy and also for the upkeep of some great estates in the north of England that they should continue to do so.

Another point in favour of the August-September season for visiting Scotland is that it coincides with a number of Highland Games meetings, especially the Braemar event which the Queen and her family usually drive the ten miles from Balmoral Castle to watch. Tossing the caber (a tall tree-trunk lopped of its branches), throwing the hammer and putting the shot are the traditional trials of strength and skill at these gatherings, varied with contests in piping and Highland dancing. Caber-tossing is nothing if not spectacular. The technique is not easily mastered and perfection is seldom attained. It is on record that the longest of the pine logs made ready for use at Braemar has been successfully tossed only three times. No wonder: it is some 19½ feet long—or tall, when held upright in the competitor's clasped hands and resting against his shoulder. To register

B oats at Oban's south pier are silhouetted here against the afterglow of sunset over the bay: just one more aspect of the infinite visual pleasure which a fortunate commingling of sea, sky and situation enables this favourite resort on the Argyllshire coast to provide.

OVERLEAF
A view of sheep grazing peacefully near the Quiraing Pass in Skye prompts the reflection that centuries ago, in the rough old times of rapacious feuding between MacDonalds and MacLeods, Quiraing was a haven of a different kind, into which cattle were driven during forays.

25

100 per cent, this massive burden must be hurled upwards and forwards in a single powerful thrust so as to pivot on its top end, complete an arc of 180 degrees, and land pointing directly away from the thrower.

The Northern Meeting Games, a two-day event on its own park close by Inverness Cathedral followed each evening by a full-dress ball in its own assembly rooms, was at one time even more aristocratic and fashionable than the Braemar Gathering. The balls have long since gone—the assembly rooms became, of all things, a social security centre—and the Games, too, lapsed for many a year. Fortunately, the event was revived in September 1984 at its original venue and there are hopes that in due course it will regain its former status in the sporting and social calendar.

The piping competitions which have been for 200 years a tradition of the Meeting have happily survived in their glory year after year. They are nowadays held at the Eden Court Theatre, an entertainment and conference centre of contemporary design not far from the Northern Meeting Park, and are recognized world-wide as the premier competitive festival of classical music of the Highland bagpipe, the ceòl mór (great music) or pibroch. It is not unusual for pipers to come from the United States, Canada and the Antipodes to compete and for enthusiasts to travel many hundreds or even thousands of miles for the pleasure of hearing them.

Some of the compositions set as test pieces have come down intact from the MacCrimmons, hereditary pipers to the MacLeods of Dunvegan in Skye. A MacCrimmon Memorial stands proudly at Boreraig on the western shore of Loch Dunvegan, above the hallowed ruins of the famous College of Piping which those master pipers established three or four centuries ago.

Over and above the unique distinction it derives from being the ancestral home of the MacCrimmons and the MacLeods, Skye is a Western Isle of mystic glamour and scenic beauty which cries out to be visited in its own right. It has been well said that no one who has never set foot on Skye can claim to know Scotland. Dennis Hardley has done well to offer us two glimpses of the magic island's varied charms—in his studies of the majestic Cuillins (p. **101**) and, by way of contrast, a haven where sheep may safely graze near the Quiraing Pass, Kilmuir (pp. **26-27**).

For pipers *en masse* the Highland Gathering to visit is the event held annually at Dunoon, an easily accessible seaside resort on the Cowal peninsula of Argyll. It attracts an entry of at least 150 bands of pipes and drums—something like 15 'hundred pipers an' a' an' a'", to adapt the old song—and the grand march as they parade is a blaze of colourful tartans and dazzling silver accoutrements as well as a mighty river of rhythmic, all-pervasive sound.

As one who has had the good fortune to hear truly great pipers like John MacDonald or George Maclennan, comparable in their own genre with Kreisler or Menuhin in theirs, few expressions seem to me more inappropriate than 'the skirl of the pipes'. There is nothing shrill or 'skirlish' about a perfectly tuned bagpipe, its chanter reed and drone reeds in absolute balance, played with faultless fingering and tonal quality by a master piper whose sole concern, lost in his music, is to interpret the sheer beauty of a tune he loves and cherishes.

Visitors to Scotland who appreciate fine music in all its forms should seize any chance to hear a really first-class piper. They still exist, especially among pipe-majors of Highland regiments who have graduated from the Army School of Piping in Edinburgh.

Another kind of music native to Scotland is the strathspey and reel, played on the fiddle either solo or in unison. As it happens, my father was a very fair violinist of semi-professional standard who knew Scott Skinner, the celebrated composer and executant of strathspeys and reels, and well-nigh idolized him. So these delightfully melodious and sprightly dance tunes were constantly practised in our house, often in duets with Alec Grant, a farmer whose fingers, you'd have thought, were too blunt and stocky to master their intricate variations.

Incidentally, there was on television a few years ago a programme in which Sir Yehudi Menuhin, visiting Scotland, was ecstatic in his admiration of a performance given by a large band of amateur fiddlers representing the Strathspey and Reel Society. Other music-loving visitors to Scotland would do well to enjoy a similarly exhilarating experience if they can.

One cannot get any farther south in Scotland than the Mull of Galloway, the extremity shown here which is only 22 miles from the Isle of Man. Galloway, a collective name for Wigtownshire and Kirkcudbrightshire, differs so markedly from the rest of Scotland as almost to form a delightfully relaxed and self-sufficient province of its own.

Scotland is admittedly a small nation in terms of population. At the most recent census (1981) its total number of residents was 5,130,735, of whom 51 per cent were women or girls. But it's a mistake to think of Scotland as a small country geographically. The mainland measures 275 miles from north to south, with a maximum width of 154 miles excluding Orkney, Shetland, the Western Isles and the well-nigh innumerable islets around the coast. The total land area adds up to 30,414 square miles, virtually one-third of the surface of Great Britain as a whole.

Yet Scotsmen find that some English people who have never been there are inclined to think of this big country as a minor neighbourly appendage, somewhere vaguely to the north of Carlisle and Newcastle upon Tyne, where everybody is quite likely to come across everybody else. On being introduced and hearing your accent, your new acquaintance will say: 'I have a second cousin in Glasgow' (or Edinburgh, Aberdeen, Oban, Perth, Elgin or wherever) 'called Sandy McIver' (which they usually pronounce as if it rhymed with 'survivor' not 'retriever'). 'I wonder if you've met him.'

This implicit assumption of parochialism is amusing rather than irritating. But it can be keenly resented by Scottish Nationalists who, proud of their nationhood, take it as covertly patronizing ignorance. The Scots have for many years evinced an almost militant pride, perhaps sometimes verging on undue self-esteem, in their national identity and in the ethical and cultural heritage they share. It is implicit in the traditional roistering challenge 'Wha's like us?' and its riposte: 'Damn'd few, and they're a' deid.'

But the politically orientated, separatist brand of nationalism is a comparatively modern phenomenon which has developed within my own lifetime. Though I can scarcely believe it now, my father always gave our home address as 'Inverness, N.B.' Perhaps there are still a few Englishmen who address their letters to 'North Britain'. But any Scotsman who did so nowadays would risk being accused of a calculated insult to his own country.

No one, even if he has lived North of the Border all his life, can honestly claim to know every square mile of the mainland, let alone all the islands. To attempt such an Odyssey, 'had we but world enough, and time', would be a lifelong adventure well worth the wearing out of countless pairs of boots. But I fancy that most of us are content to leave the trudging to the indispensable topographers of the Ordnance Survey, whose accurate maps and faithfully sited triangulation marks have put many an erring wayfarer in their debt.

Highland stravaigers may even forgive them for having unwittingly profaned with one of those utilitarian marks the exact site in Glenelg, on the mainland directly across from Skye, of the remains of an ancient cairn dedicated to the Clan MacCrimmon. I am told that traces of this relic from the brave days of old may still be found on its hilltop not very far from what is left of Bernera Barracks. This establishment housed Hanoverian soldiers until the last decade of the eighteenth century, by which time the Jacobite rising had become a fairly distant memory.

As to Glenelg itself, I wonder whether children in Scotland are still able to answer correctly when asked to point out a peculiar feature of the

Sweetheart Abbey—could one imagine a more romantic name for a religious foundation? Balliol men have even better reason than most to honour its founder, Devorgilla, for in addition to dedicating the thirteenth-century abbey to the memory of her husband John Balliol she founded the Oxford college in his name. The ruined abbey, seven miles south of Dumfries on A710, owes much of its distinctive beauty to the delicate shade of pink sandstone, the product of sand from the nearby River Nith, of which it was built. One cannot but think of Petra, the 'rose-red city half as old as time'.

name. In my day most boys and girls would say, 'Please, miss, you can spell it the same way backwards as forwards.' But a Ross-shire teacher recently told me that a new girl in her class, who had just been transferred from a school in England, astonished everyone by replying 'It's a palindrome'. Alas, when invited to explain what a palindrome was she added 'A theatre in London'.

Undoubtedly the best way to acquaint oneself with Scotland is on foot. But for the average holiday-maker, with no longer than, say, a month to spare for his entire visit, this is a counsel of unattainable perfection. Next best, perhaps, come bicycle or horseback (ample facilities for pony-trekking are available in Scotland) but these modes of transport depend on the rider's physical aptitude and endurance, not to mention the reliability of his mount.

Most visitors to Scotland nowadays travel in their own family cars or rented ones. This is all very well if the driver has a wife or other passenger who can take a spell at the wheel; otherwise he is liable, by rightly concentrating on his driving, to miss quite a lot of the scenic beauty he has come to see. So far as road transport is concerned, my personal preference would be either to join a coach tour, of which there is plenty of choice, or else take a pre-planned series of the scheduled bus services with which many parts of Scotland, thanks to new and improved roads, are now fairly well networked.

It was of course the Railway Age of the mid-nineteenth century which first opened up Scotland to what we now know as tourism. As late as my boyhood only the very well-to-do had cars of their own. The 1920s were well advanced before most Invernessians thought of travelling to Edinburgh or Glasgow, let alone to London, by any means other than the train.

The Highland Railway, with its headquarters and main workshops in Inverness, we regarded as our very own. Every schoolboy along the line from Perth northwards could identify its green-liveried locomotives—often named after Bens, Glens or Lochs—as they laboriously hauled their heavy-laden trains up to and over the summit at Dalnaspidal. I'm reminded of a typical example of the dry, dead-pan humour relished by literal-minded Scots. Awaiting at Inverness the arrival of a passenger from Aberdeen, a friend of mine asked a porter 'How long will the Aberdeen train be?' Came the reply: 'Eight coaches and a van'.

True to the Civil Service draftsman's notion of the perfect Parliamentary answer, it was brief, it was accurate and it told the questioner nothing he hadn't known before.

The richly carved Norman church faithfully represented here is by no means the only claim to fame of Leuchars in East Fife. As the railway junction for St Andrews six miles away, Leuchars Station for many years, before the building of the Forth and Tay road bridges, monopolized high and mighty travellers of the academic and golfing worlds. The church, with its original chancel and apse, is reckoned among Scotland's finest Norman buildings.

Merged first in the LMS (London, Midland & Scottish) and then in the nationalized British Railways, the old Highland Railway didn't fare particularly well under either dispensation. But there are signs that it is at last coming into its own as Highland Rail, a self-contained division of the still-nationalized undertaking. Inverness Station, in the very heart of the Capital of the Highlands, has been re-modelled as one of the most attractive and convenient in the entire BR system, and the service in its

As shown here, the village or township of Arrochar stands at the head of Loch Long within the Argyll National Park. Yet it is only 25 miles from Dumbarton with its shipyards and factories.

well-equipped and staffed bar and buffet equals any I have ever encountered.

Perhaps rail freight may never regain the predominance it knew in the days when coal was king of motive power, but Highland Rail's policy of combining bargain prices with skilful marketing seems to be paying off so far as passenger traffic is concerned. Some of the bus services are being beaten at their own game, in that trains are catering for local commuters as well as long-distance travellers.

I have dwelt on the subject of railways partly out of nostalgia but also to make the point that it might be worth choosing to do much of your sight-seeing in Scotland by train. There are in particular at least two routes of scenic splendour where there is no acceptable alternative to rail because many of the mountains and lochs you will view in comfort from the train are not accessible by road.

First, the West Highland Line from Glasgow via Fort William to Mallaig (164 miles). The very station names along the way smack of

Scotland — Ardlui, Rannoch, Locheilside, Lochailort. Early in its journey
the train runs between Loch Long and Loch Lomond, two of Scotland's
noblest examples of sea-loch and freshwater-lake respectively.

   Loch Long, of which Hardley offers an autumnal impression (pp. **34-35**)
mirroring Arrochar at its head, is typical of numerous inlets on the
west coast where the sea cuts into the land. Why most of them should be
called sea-lochs, whereas inlets on the east coast are nearly always known
as firths, is a difference I can't explain. Nor is it easy to account for the fact
that a genuine and completely authentic sea-loch on the north
coast is named the Kyle of Tongue, whereas the word 'kyle' also means a
narrow channel between mainland and island, as in Kyle of Lochalsh or
the Kyles of Bute. But there is no quirk of nomenclature to cast doubt on
the primacy of Loch Lomond, 23 miles long and 27½ square miles in area,
as Scotland's largest expanse of fresh water entirely contained within its
own 'bonny, bonny banks'.

   Later, wending northwards via Crianlarich, the West Highland route

This wintry projection across Loch Rannoch is notable for its unusual peacefulness. Loch and Moor could scarcely be relied upon for many winter days of such relative calm. Schiehallion, seen in the distance to the east, is a dramatic mountain rising to 3547 feet.

crosses Rannoch Moor, reputed scene of poor David Balfour's ordeals in *Kidnapped*. The aspect of the moor which Hardley has chosen (pp. **36-37**), gazing across Loch Rannoch towards Schiehallion's distinctive peak, suggests that winter can lend a certain enchantment to its bleakness on a calm, sunlit day. As it nears Fort William the train affords a magnificent view of Ben Nevis (4406 feet), the highest mountain in the British Isles, though only one among 276 peaks over 3000 feet in Scotland. These, incidentally, are known in the climbing fraternity as 'Munros', a category which commemorates the mountaineer, Sir Hugh Munro, who first defined and counted them. Hence, too, the expression 'Munro-bagger' to denote a climber whose intent is to scale them one and all.

Fort William is itself a pleasant and welcoming town on the shores of Loch Linnhe, but it would be a pity to end one's journey there without taking advantage of the last leg of the West Highland Line for at least a day-trip to Mallaig. This busy fishing port is reached by a mainly waterside route which some seasoned travellers esteem the most scenically rewarding in the whole domain of British Rail.

The train is carried Mallaig-wards by the Glenfinnan Viaduct, one of a number of remarkable civil-engineering feats in Scotland—still in daily use—which give you cause to marvel at the confident expertise of Victorian railway surveyors and architects, not to mention the physical strength and endurance of the humble navvies who wrought manfully to translate those great men's designs into stone and steel.

From the viaduct, overlooking the head of Loch Shiel, one has an excellent view of the Glenfinnan Monument, of which Hardley has provided a magnificent and memorable impression, lit by the westering sun. This lofty circular tower near the loch shore, surmounted by the statue of a clansman, identifies the place where Italy-born Charles Edward Louis Philip Sylvester Casimir Maria Stuart ('Bonnie Prince Charlie'), son of the 'Old Pretender', raised his standard in August 1745 amidst, it is said, as many as 3000 Highlanders who had espoused his claim to the British throne.

A visitor centre close at hand tells the sorry tale of the aspirant monarch's initially successful advance as far south as Derby, in central England, and then the despairing retreat to the débacle of Culloden, where the fond dream of kingship weltered to its extinction in clansmen's blood scarcely nine months after the glory and glamour of Glenfinnan.

About 70 years later the Monument was erected by a pious Macdonald of Glenaladale, whether out of suppressed sympathy with the Prince's cause or determination that the wanton waste of human life should never be forgotten I cannot say. At all events, there it stands, I hope for centuries to come. As a Highlander, I weep a little in my heart at sight of it.

You may cross by ferry from Mallaig to Armadale, near the southern tip of the Isle of Skye, but on the whole I'd prefer to keep Skye as the *pièce de résistance* at journey's end of the other rail-borne treat I'm recommending. This is the Kyle Line from Inverness, created in the early years of this century and better patronized today, I'm told, than ever before. If you intend taking a morning train in high summer it would be prudent to reserve a seat, lest you have to stand with other holiday-makers bound for Muir of Ord or for Dingwall, the Junction for places to

It is seldom one sees a monument to failure, but such is the sad truth about the Glenfinnan tower commemorating the raising of Bonnie Prince Charlie's standard at the head of Loch Shiel in August 1745. There is a visitor centre nearby to tell the sorry tale, redeemed only by the astonishing bravery, endurance and loyalty of Highlanders such as the clansman whose effigy surmounts the tower. The site is about 18 miles west of Fort William.

OVERLEAF

The wide bay around whose curving shores men began to build their habitations countless centuries ago is still one of Oban's many assets as a holiday resort. Others include a mild climate and an unusually long 'season'. The bay makes the town an ideal yachting centre and also a convenient point of departure for ferry services and day trips round islands such as Mull, Iona, Staffa, Coll, Tiree, to name but a few. And the hilly background, as this picture shows, can enhance the view even after nightfall.

the north such as Alness, Invergordon and Tain.

After leaving Inverness by a swing bridge over the River Ness and the Caledonian Canal, the train wanders at a comparatively leisurely pace, ideal for photography, through some of the most picturesque glens, each with its sparkling stream or shimmering loch, and alongside some of the most awesome bens, whether rocky or heather-clad, to be found in all Scotland. The wayside station names are a litany of Highlandry, if one may coin a word: Lochluichart, Achanalt, Achnasheen, Achnashellach, Strathcarron, Attadale, Stromeferry, Duncraig, Plockton and Duirinish.

As it nears the terminus at Kyle of Lochalsh the track runs roughly parallel with a lagoon whose waters, in contrast with the white sands below, seem to take on an almost Mediterranean blue. Kyle is a hospitable wee township with good hotels, guest-houses and caravan sites, and it makes an excellent base from which to tour Glen Shiel or Strathcarron. But there is no doubt that Kyle's main attraction is its proximity to Skye, which can be reached at the busy little port of Kyleakin in a few minutes by a frequent ferry service across Loch Alsh.

With Portree and Broadford, Kyleakin ranks as one of the three main urban areas of the island. It is pronounced, by the way, as Kyle-*aw*-kin, with the accent on the middle syllable. The 'kin' suffix recalls Viking times when the native Skyemen had to keep watch on the Inner Sound of Raasay for the advent of marauding Norse longships.

Mention of Raasay, the long island off the eastern coast of Skye, reminds me that recently, lunching in a Knightsbridge bar, my wife and I were joined by a middle-aged couple who had arrived at London Airport that morning from their home in Virginia. They informed us that this was their tenth annual visit and that after a few days' shopping they would be leaving, as usual, for Scotland—to be precise, for Raasay. A long and difficult journey? Not at all, I was told. 'You fly from Heathrow to Glasgow, catch a flight from there to Broadford in Skye, and then it's only 10 or 12 miles along the coastal road round the head of Loch Ainort to Sconser, where you get the ferry for Raasay.'

It was clear that the American was very well informed about this outlying part of my own country. The reason soon emerged. He was a 'Mac' who had traced his family line through several United States-born generations to its origin in Raasay. His wife, though not herself of Scottish descent, shared his enthusiasm for the island and the clan. They were at one in their ambition to settle permanently somewhere on Raasay when the husband retired from his executive post in a Wall Street firm. Other interests, he said, would still require him to visit the United States occasionally. But he foresaw no problem in fulfilling that obligation from a Hebridean island base. 'Provided you can afford to fly, no two places in the civilized world are inaccessible from each other. And the telephone, radio and satellite television, not to mention computerized updates of what's happening in money and stock markets world-wide, will make it just about as easy to keep an eye on financial affairs from Skye as from an office in London or New York.'

A stimulating conversation. But I couldn't help thinking it rather a pity that modern communications in their various forms had overtaken the lines beloved of Scottish singers:

From the lone shieling of the misty island
Mountains divide us and a waste of seas;
Yet still the blood is strong, the heart is
    Highland,
And we in dreams behold the Hebrides.

Countless St Andrew's societies and Burns societies all over the world testify to the existence of millions of people—some of them black, as in Jamaica, where Robert Burns himself at one time intended to settle—who glory in their Scots descent. It says something for the durability of the Scottish ethos of piety, independence, concern for the family, thrift, education and self-improvement that it has persisted so long and so far away.

A few years ago Lord Duncan-Sandys, learning that I hailed from Inverness, recalled that on his first visit to New Zealand as Commonwealth Relations Secretary (1960-64) he made a point of seeking out the place where a forebear of his mother's named Cameron, emigrating from the Highlands in the mid-nineteenth century, had founded a successful sheep farm. He was taken to Cameron's original homestead, little better than a rough-hewn log cabin, which had been preserved as a showpiece.

The interior walls had been lined with sheets of newspaper, then coated with some concoction which helped to bind them together and keep out the worst of the wind and the rain. The Secretary of State's eye was caught by a scrap of paper on which he could make out the title *Inverness Courier* and a date in 1856. Presumably the newspapers had been mailed to Cameron by family or friends to keep him in touch with the homeland, though the contents must have been history rather than news by the time they reached him.

My father spent his working life on the *Courier*, which after his premature death became the *alma mater* in journalism of myself and a younger brother in turn, and I was delighted to hear of this link with its illustrious past.

I don't know whether the Victorian Mr Cameron, having made a fortune through New Zealand wool, mutton and lamb, ever returned to his native Highlands; but now two-way traffic between Scottish expatriates and their relatives at home is greater than ever before. The aeroplane is of course largely responsible for this.

Dwellers in the remoter parts of Scotland have certainly been beneficiaries of air travel. The Inner and Outer Hebrides are fairly well served with miniature airports or landing strips, and communications with and between the Northern Isles (Orkney and Shetland) have gained in this respect from the requirements of the North Sea oil industry. Seven of the small airports in the Highlands and Islands are controlled by the Civil Aviation Authority, which is also responsible for investing £30,000,000 or more in improvements at Sumburgh in the Shetlands.

Mainly because of oil industry traffic, Aberdeen has become one of the

This springtime view across the
Sound of Jura towards the long
Island of that name was taken from a
point near Kilberry, at the southern
end of the Knapdale peninsula in
Argyllshire. The Island, almost
severed at its waistline by the
intrusive Loch Tarbert, is notable for
its wealth of streams and hills, rising
to about 2500 feet with the Paps of
Jura.

S ad to say, ruined churches are by no means rare sights nowadays. But the old Free Kirk at Gaskalone, Inverness-shire is of special note because it was built of locally quarried granite.

world's biggest and busiest helicopter ports. The throughput of Scottish airports as a whole has recently been recorded at something around 7,000,000 passengers a year. Thanks to keen competition between private enterprise and the State-owned airline, fares are gradually being pared to the point at which internal air travel may yet become as popular with the British public as 'package tours' to resorts in Europe and many other parts of the world have been for years.

North Sea oil, the first of which was brought ashore as recently as in 1975, has made Aberdeen 'an' twal' mile roond', as they say, the most prosperous urban community in Scotland, possibly in all Britain except, one may guess, the 'Square Mile' around the Bank of England. Known for generations as the Granite City, from the sun-catching sparkle of the locally quarried igneous rock of which many of its prominent buildings are constructed, it is nowadays known also as the oil capital of Europe or sometimes as Scotland's own Texas.

The Grampians and the Cairngorms are rich in granite rocks, some containing semi-precious stones such as the tawny-yellow or wine-hued cairngorm (hence its name). In Crathie Church, where members of the Royal Family worship when in residence on Deeside, the pulpit is built of 18 different kinds of granite, all Scottish.

Leaving aside 'Dallas' and all that, the authentic State of Texas must have a genuine affinity with Aberdeen over and above mutual interest in the oil industry. It claims that its population of Scottish descent exceeds the number of Scots actually living in Scotland. Moreover, its monumental domed granite capitol in the city of Austin was built by Scottish stonemasons brought over for the purpose.

As I write, Austin is reported to be planning to stage annual Highland gatherings with all the time-honoured trimmings—pipers, dancers, caber-tossers and so on—plus a mile race run in the kilt (let us hope trews are also mandatory). No doubt there will also be a parade of folk heroes like Davy Crockett (of the coonskin cap), James Bowie (of the knife), Sam Houston (the state's first governor) and Stephen F. Austin, in whose honour the capital was named. All four were of Scottish descent; there are certainly many born Scotsmen bearing similar surnames in Scotland to this day.

For many years Aberdeen, with its extensive sandy beach, attractive parks and busy, colourful harbour, has been a favourite holiday resort for Scottish families—perhaps especially because its landladies have always been noted for giving good value. Now that the city is more accessible than ever, by several air services as well as train, bus and car, increasing numbers of visitors from England and overseas are making it a convenient start-point for tours of the scenic interior and coastline of north-east Scotland, Caithness and the Northern Isles (as Orkney, Shetland and their numerous satellites are collectively known).

Aberdeen as a sight-seeing base is hard to match for the variety it offers at all seasons and at ranges to suit. For example, one may be tempted by Hardley's spirited view of the rugged cliffs fringing the Bay of Cruden to travel 20-odd miles North of the city to the impressive ruins of Slains Castle (p. **48**) stark in a pastoral setting. This would then be the cue for a visit to Cruden Bay village, an 'away from it all' resort which the former

Viewed here from the south, Slains Castle near Cruden Bay on the Buchan coast looks impressively venerable. But its extensive ruins are those of a castle founded in 1664 to replace an even earlier namesake at the other (southern) end of the bay. Extended and rebuilt by the 9th Earl of Errol— whose descendant, the 23rd Countess, holds also the hereditary title of Lady Slains—the 'new' Slains Castle had the distinction of a visit by Dr Johnson and Boswell in 1773. The nearby village of Port Errol takes its name from the earldom.

A misty morning seems to suit the sturdy character of Stonehaven, the county town of Kincardineshire on the rugged North Sea coast. True to its name, it boasts many dwellings built of stone which have proved real havens for generations of families. Archaeologists consider the town an interesting example of a seventeenth-century Scottish community.

OVERLEAF
This view across Stonehaven harbour at dusk shows that the town built next to the sea remains in essence a seafaring community. But its fishing industry today is perhaps of less importance to the local economy than the thriving holiday trade for which it caters with increasing success.

North British railway company fostered by establishing a station which would also serve their own luxury hotel and thus lure the well-to-do from England for a spell of peace, quiet and golf. Bram Stoker of 'Dracula' fame was one who evidently found the village way of life conducive to the weaving of his Gothic fantasies.

Should you prefer a coastal excursion somewhere south of the city, a 20-mile drive in that direction would take you to Dunnottar Castle, a ruined yet menacing fortress atop a cliff 160 feet above the North Sea. A stronghold of the Earls Marischal of Scotland from the fourteenth century, Dunnottar became during the Commonwealth wars the secret repository of the Honours of Scotland (the Scottish regalia). Though Cromwell's soldiers besieged and occupied the Castle, the Crown jewels were smuggled out in 1651 by the intrepid wife of the parish minister of Kinneff, seven miles southwards along the coast. The faithful pastor, James Granger, managed to conceal them for nine years under the pulpit and flagstones of his kirk. There is a memorial to him in the present building, which dates only from 1738. On the way back to Aberdeen as daylight was waning one might have the luck to see the pleasant resort and fishing port of Stonehaven as Hardley saw it in what one might call his 'Ellingtonian' study in indigo and deep purple (pp. **52-53**). But you would have to re-visit this sturdy, aptly named town (mainly stone-built) in the afternoon if you wished to inspect its quayside Tolbooth Museum, a sixteenth-century building which was originally the Earls Marischals' storehouse and later became a prison.

Aberdeen itself has such a wealth of treats to enjoy that the visitor may be tempted to spend an entire vacation within its municipal boundary. It has all the sophistication and amenities of a major capital; luxury hotels and restaurants; fashionable stores and boutiques; an ancient university of world repute; a discerningly stocked art gallery; a commodious concert hall; a beautiful theatre offering productions of West End standard; Scotland's champion football club; even a regimental headquarters ('the plucky wee Gordon's the pride o' them a').

Among the city's most popular assets, surprisingly enough for somewhere open to winds from the allegedly bleak North Sea, are its flowers. Nowhere will you find in spring a more luxuriant carpeting of crocuses and daffodils, and from early summer to mid-autumn the roses are fabulous in their abundance and in the quality of their multi-hued blooms. Perhaps without realizing it you may see scions of that noble line in many countries, for the celebrated rose-growers of Aberdeen do a big export trade, worthily upholding the traditional fame of the old Scottish gardener.

I should in fairness point out that Aberdeen has its rivals for floral beauty elsewhere in Scotland, and not only in cultivated gardens. For vivid colour you can seldom beat nature herself, as witness the golden broom blazing its way along many a roadside verge or railway embankment; or the heliotrope or deeper purple foxgloves of Inverness-shire and Argyllshire; or — perhaps queen of all — the glorious flowering of the heather on vast stretches of moorland in August and September.

Hardley has provided us with three examples, from widely separate parts of Scotland, of the formal garden at its most attractive. The tailored,

Mellerstain House in Berwickshire, between Kelso and Galashiels, is among the most beautiful mansions in Scotland open to the public. The interior decoration and plasterwork are particularly fine. No wonder: the original architect in 1725 was William Adam and the house was completed about 50 years later by his son Robert. But for all the Adamses' celebrated skills in design and craftsmanship, many a visitor may find even more charming the fairy tale scene, pictured here, at the Tea House in the grounds.

The Isle of Arran claims to be 'Scotland in Miniature' and the colourful gardens of Brodick Castle, with a country park noted for its rhododendrons, are among its many attractions. Once the seat of the Dukes of Hamilton, the Castle houses some fine silver, porcelain and paintings. Brodick is the port for the ferry from Ardrossan, only an hour's sailing distant on the Ayrshire coast.

hedge-bound, many-flowered beds around the whimsical teahouse at Mellerstain, Berwickshire (p. **54**); the well-drilled full-dress parade of blooms, lawns and shrubs marching towards a vista of conifers at Brodick Castle, Arran (pp. **56-57**); and the gay miscellany of crimson, green and gold that greets the spring in Rouken Glen Park, a great credit to Glasgow.

Because of Scotland's distance from London and other large centres of population in England, its tourist trade would almost certainly benefit from a growth of internal air travel at reasonable fares. A large-scale

R ouken Glen, whose beautiful walled gardens are shown here, is but one of more than 70 public parks within the Greater Glasgow area. It is also among the best-loved of them all, perhaps because, situated south-west of the city approximately between Thornliebank and Newton Mearns, it gives the visitor a delightful sense of being 'in the country'.

Strone Gardens alongside the eastern shores of Loch Fyne, Argyllshire, near the head of that great sea loch, were the pride and joy of their laird, the late Lord Glenkinlas. A former Secretary for Scotland as Michael Noble, MP, he took his title from the home glen he loved. The gardens, shown here in spring-time, are open to the public from April to September. They are noted for daffodils, primulas, exotic shrubs and rhododendrons. Their Pinetum—the area devoted to pines and other conifers—contains what is said to be the tallest tree in Britain.

OVERLEAF

A peaceful scene among the reeds of the Crinan Canal, Argyllshire, reminds us that nearly 200 years have gone by since the nine-mile canal between Crinan sea-loch and Ardrishaig, via Loch-gilphead, was built to enable shipping to move from Loch Fyne to the Atlantic without having to round the long peninsula of Kintyre. Its traffic nowadays is mostly pleasure craft.

development of 'package tours' from abroad might be of even greater advantage to Scotland's economy. However, there is very little danger of Scotland's becoming 'over-run' with tourists. As was pointed out in an earlier chapter, it is a big country, with many thousands of acres virtually untrodden by man. The Highland region—about one-third of the total area of Scotland—has a density of fewer than eight people per square kilometre. Four-fifths of Scotland's people live in the cities, towns and villages of the industrialized central belt.

Most of the foreign journalists with whom I worked seem to have found Scottish people friendly and helpful, especially in hotels and guest-houses. 'Much more approachable than the English', they said. Of course, they may have tactfully said much the same thing in reverse to English colleagues. The fact remains that for strictly economic reasons Scotland needs to attract more and more visitors. The evidence is only too convincing that the 'heavy' industries—iron and steel, coal, shipbuilding, bridge-building, railway engineering—which once made it a major workshop of the world are in serious decline. Belated attempts to re-establish Scottish car and truck-making industries have largely failed.

It is true that a switch in recent years towards lighter engineering products has been successful and Scotland is now said to have the biggest concentration of the electronic industry in Western Europe, with over 200 companies including a number financed from the United States and Japan. This sector, employing more than 40,000 men and women, has helped Scotland to improve its manufacturing productivity, with a growth rate in 1984 of 8.5 per cent—nearly double that of the United Kingdom as a whole. But what has really helped to offset the cyclical decline in employment elsewhere in the Scottish economy is the fact that in the six years to mid-1984 jobs in the 'services' sector increased by 81,000. The sector now accounts for 65 per cent of the total workforce and is one area of sustained employment growth. Tourism is a service industry *par excellence*. The basic attractions are already there in abundance. Nature has been prodigal in providing Scotland with facilities for an almost infinite variety of sports and recreations, whether on land or water, in summer or winter.

Let me list a few at random: mountaineering and hill walking; bird watching; pony trekking; trout and salmon fishing on some of the best rivers in the British Isles, if not the world; deer-stalking and grouse, pheasant and partridge shooting in season; curling on indoor rinks, or outdoors when frost permits; sea fishing almost anywhere off 6300 miles of mainland and island coastline, which also offers numerous clean, unspoilt beaches, of pebbly shingle or fine sand; yachting and sailing on famous oceanic waters like the Firth of Clyde or on many a land-girt loch.

Above all, golf. No one seems to dispute that the world's most widely practised game originated in Scotland five centuries ago. Certainly the writ of the Royal and Ancient Golf Club at St Andrews, most celebrated among Scotland's more than 400 courses, runs unchallenged as the international governing body of the game.

Jack Nicklaus, still Britain's favourite among American golfers, left no doubt about his preference for Scotland when he came over, as usual, for the 1985 open championship.

This view across the harbour of Carradale towards the faraway hills of Arran conveys the tranquillity which is the charm of this quiet little resort on the east coast of the Mull of Kintyre. It is notable for the walled and wild gardens of Carradale House, at their best in spring and early summer.

OVERLEAF

The charming seaside town of Largs, only 30 miles by car from Glasgow, is probably the favourite in a string of holiday resorts along the eastern shores of the Firth of Clyde. This splendid view from one of the town's two golf courses indicates how well planned it is. A magnificent outlook seaward across the Cumbraes is complemented by a mild climate and ample amenities, including steamer trips, sailing and sea-fishing.

65

Thisunset silhouette of
St Andrews Cathedral, the noble
remains of the twelfth-century
edifice with which the world-
famous royal burgh in north-east
Fife shares the name of Scotland's
patron saint, is even more dramatic
than a similar view in full daylight.
Nearly 400 feet long, it was once the
largest church in Scotland.

'I like all the British Open venues', he said diplomatically. 'But I would
put Muirfield and St Andrews first and then Turnberry and Troon. After
that I would work my way down to England.'

Another factor worth bearing in mind, though probably of no great
concern to Mr Nicklaus, is that the green fees for visitors at Scottish
courses, championship courses included, are reckoned to be just about the
best value available in the golfing world.

It will have been clear already that I have a soft side for Aberdeen. Such
is equally true of Pitlochry, which struck me as a charming little town
when I first saw it more than half a century ago on a day trip from
Dundee and which I have found more and more attractive on every visit
since. It has grown, of course, but in an almost imperceptible way, with
little or no concession to stark and aggressive modernity. This can as justly
be said of the big hotels as of the houses and shops. They all seem to have
the knack of looking as if they were native to their Highland environment.

Some of those shops, by the way, especially those devoted to luxury
trades such as jewellery or high fashion, are as 'smart' as you will find in

Bond Street or Knightsbridge. That fine old purveyor of yesteryear, the 'family grocer and Italian warehouseman', also seems to have survived in Pitlochry. And they still contrive to stock special delicacies which have long since vanished from the shelves of city supermarkets.

A glance at the map will show that if any town can claim to be at or near the centre of Scotland it is Pitlochry astride the River Tummel. On journeys homeward from London it always seemed to me to be the real beginning of the Highlands, even though Perth is rightly known as the Gateway. Open the train or car window and you sense an indefinable difference in the air; Queen Victoria's physician called it the finest and most bracing air in all Europe.

Sixty years ago or thereabouts there was bitter opposition in the Highlands, chiefly on amenity grounds, to the proposed development of hydro-electric power. But Pitlochry must be thankful that the schemes eventually went ahead. There are now nine hydro stations in the Tummel Valley, and the town owes to a Hydro Board-constructed dam the creation of Loch Faskally, which fits beautifully into the landscape as if it had been exactly where it is since the dawn of time. Moreover, it has the added advantage, from a sightseer's point of view, of a good road all the way round.

Last time a friend took me there we stopped for lunch at an attractive roadside inn commanding an excellent view of the loch. The hospitable young couple who kept the pub turned out to be Australians who had been so captivated by the Highlands on a holiday visit some years earlier that they determined to acquire a business which would enable them to spend the rest of their lives within easy reach of Pitlochry.

The combination of a dam regulating the flow from Loch Faskally with a specially constructed salmon 'ladder' just a short walk from the town centre enables Pitlochry to treat townspeople and tourists to a fascinating aquatic display. The Salmon Leap has become a major free attraction for ecologists and anglers from many countries. Salmon spawned in the streams above the dam duly make their way downstream, out to the open sea and thence all the way to the Atlantic for the next phase in their lives. Years later, driven by the homing impulse of their species, they return to Scotland seeking the actual spawning-grounds where their lives began. Were it not for the ascending ladder, 900 feet from base to top, they would have no hope of getting past the power station and swimming on through the dam to their journey's end. Thanks to Hydro Board goodwill, an observation chamber is available which enables visitors to see for themselves the powerful fish leaping clear of their natural element as they mount from grade to grade of the ladder. Of course they don't perform to order and a patient wait may be necessary. But when it happens the leap—the sudden flash of a silvery, arched body shimmering in the sunlight—is worth its place in any photographer's collection.

The site of another celebrated jump, though one scarcely as well attested as those of the salmon, can be seen at the Pass of Killiecrankie, a wooded gorge four miles north of Pitlochry. Known as the 'Soldier's Leap', this owes its name to the legend that in 1689—when English troops were put to flight at Killiecrankie by a Jacobite force under the leadership

The sylvan beauty of this view of the Pass of Killiecrankie on the River Garry above Pitlochry is a reminder of grim and stirring times. In 1689 it was the scene of the legendary Soldier's Leap but also of the death in battle of 'Bonnie Dundee', Graham of Claverhouse.

of 'Bonnie Dundee' (Graham of Claverhouse)—a soldier hard-pressed to outrun pursuit leaped clean across the River Garry at a point where, I suppose, the feat is just physically possible.

But the Garry is a pretty substantial river, and even when its waters are very low its west and east banks don't get any closer to each other. Still, the thought of a claymore, broadsword or pike about to pierce your vitals could lend wings, whether you'd been fighting for the exiled Stuart King James II or for his Protestant daughter Mary and her husband William of Orange.

Hardley has given us a graphic impression of the Pass and the river, looking northwards (p. **71**). What a terrain for hand-to-hand fighting! And one can see that the Leap must indeed have been a formidable ordeal. Incidentally, I believe it is a mistake to assume that the clan chiefs and their clansmen were all faithful to one side or the other—the Jacobite side or the Hanoverian—in all three risings of 1689, 1715 and 1745. It was inevitable that personal relationships within and between clans should play their part, as well as reputed political and religious affinities with one cause or the other.

A venue about seven miles from Pitlochry, hard by the traditional Road to the Isles ('by Loch Tummel and Loch Rannoch and Lochaber I will go') is the recognised point from which to enjoy the famous 'Queen's View'. The sovereign in question was of course Victoria, whose appreciation of Scottish scenery was by no means confined to 'Dear Paradise', the term she applied to her own Balmoral estate on Deeside.

Long before acquiring Balmoral—reputedly out of a legacy of £500,000 left her by an eccentric miser—the Queen paid a number of visits to Scotland, she and the Prince Consort staying in the homes of aristocratic friends like the Breadalbanes at Taymouth Castle, the Glenlyons at Blair Atholl and the Abercorns at Ardverikie. During this period she improved her skills in draughtsmanship and watercolour under the tuition of a Glasgow-born artist, William Leighton Leitch, as well as Edward Lear and, later, Landseer, who fully shared her devotion to the Highlands.

The view named after her, down the whole length of islanded Loch Tummel to its continuation via the river, with the 3547 foot peak of Schiehallion to your left as you gaze and other heights of the Western seaboard on the horizon, is certainly one of those views which cry out to be seen. But there is such a wealth of loch, river and mountain scenery readily accessible from Pitlochry, not to mention vast areas of woodland and moorland, that it seems a trifle partial to nominate any particular viewpoint as first among equals.

One need only cite a few famous names at random: the great River Tay, at 118 miles Scotland's longest from source to sea, and its companion Loch; Glen Lyon with its rock-bound fastnesses and turbulent river; the long, narrow Loch Ericht overlooked by Ben Alder (3757 feet); Craiganour Forest on one side of Glen Garry and the Forest of Atholl on the other; Glen Truim stretching North from Dalwhinnie; Glen Tilt, Strathardle, Glenshee—the choice is almost infinite.

If one's taste inclines to characteristic old Scottish towns, there are easy excursions to Blair Atholl, distinguished by the Duke of Atholl's stately

home, Blair Castle, and his 'private army', the Atholl Highlanders; or Dunkeld with its ancient cathedral; or my own favourite Blairgowrie, built mainly of Old Red Sandstone, with its glorious Rosemount golf course, now deservedly on the championship list and esteemed by many as the most beautiful course they have ever played.

Nor should we omit Aberfeldy, where the raising in 1739 of The Black Watch, primarily to mount guard on the unruly Highlands, is commemorated by a large cairn and kilted statue near General Wade's bridge ('If you'd seen those roads before they were made, you would hold up your hands and bless General Wade'). Fortingall Churchyard, between Aberfeldy and Glen Lyon, deserves a visit if only because it contains a yew tree ascertained to be more than 3000 years old — said to be the oldest living thing (animal, vegetable or mineral) in all Europe.

By way of drawing attention to lesser-known beauties of Perthshire as they appear at different seasons of the year, Dennis Hardley has selected on the one hand an enticing view of Loch Tulla and Black Mount in spring-time (p. **77**). On the other hand he contrasts these with studies, no less attractive of their kind, of Glen Dochart, Loch Lubhair and one of the numerous Falls of Dochart, all caught in winter's icy grip.

A parting word about Pitlochry. If I were lucky enough to be there between the beginning of May and the end of September I wouldn't think of leaving without trying to book a seat at its Festival Threatre, known internationally as 'the theatre in the hills'. As indeed it is; from its windows you can look across the Tummel below to Ben Vrackie five miles away.

Founded in 1950, if one may apply that solid-sounding verb to what was initially a tented structure, this bold venture kept first-class repertory to the fore through good times and bad until it ultimately developed into one of the finest all-purpose entertainment facilities in Britain and had the distinction in 1981 of being formally opened by the Prince of Wales. West End critics love coming to review its productions — and no wonder.

From Pitlochry the tourist's progress northwards, whether by rail or the greatly improved A9 road, is easy and relatively swift, but only if he can resist various temptations to linger on the way. The first of these might be Dalwhinnie, which is about 1900 feet above sea level and houses the world's highest whisky distillery. A few miles away to the West, beyond Benalder Forest, is Loch Laggan — of which Hardley, sharing Landseer's appreciation of its wintry aspect, has photographed one view of an ice-bound waterfall on its north shore (p. **76**) and another looking across its partly frozen surface (pp. **92-93**).

Next we come to tranquil, easy-going Newtonmore, with its Clan MacPherson museum, and to busy, lively Kingussie (say 'King-*you*-see'), which has a fascinating collection of Highland folk exhibits. Those two little towns, or big villages, are near-neighbours and, passing through them in turn, one can take note of the Monadliath Mountains to the west and the mighty Grampian and Cairngorm ranges to the east, capped by the towering trio of Ben Macdui (4296 feet), Braeriach (4248 feet) and Cairntoul (4241 feet).

The Braeriach plateau, where rises the River Dee, could well be called the roof of Great Britain. Below a sheer cliff descending from the summit there is a deep corrie (steep hollow) which fills up in winter with huge

A spectacular view through the Scots pines at Black Mount, to the immediate north of Loch Tulla, Perthshire, is evidence that coniferous trees do well in Scotland, for obvious climatic reasons. But by no means all the pines one sees are relics of the old Caledonian forest, of which survivors are most likely to be found on Speyside, Deeside and Wester Ross.

OVERLEAF
This view in Glen Dochart, as seen from the shore of Loch Lubhair, twinned with its neighbour Loch Dochart, is characteristic of the winter wonderland which West Perthshire can sometimes become.

TOP LEFT

The icy waterfall which dominates this study of Loch Laggan shows that Jack Frost can be a talented sculptor. This example of his art was seen on the north-western shore, from which there are views of the distant heights of Benalder Forest.

LEFT

An unusual view of one of the many falls of the Perthshire river Dochart above Killin, where it merges with the sinuous Loch Tay, source of the mighty river which ultimately reaches the North Sea by the Firth of Tay. Killin is a pleasant little Highland town at the west end of the loch.

ABOVE

An early spring view from Black Mount across Loch Tulla, Perthshire, looks southward to the distant hills above Glen Orchy. The loch is within two or three miles of Bridge of Orchy station on the West Highland line.

77

drifts of blizzard-blown snow. The great snow-trap formed in this way
has seldom if ever been known to disappear entirely from view, even at
the height of a warm and sunny summer. Instead, the snow tends to
solidify as autumn approaches and will thus be all the better able to
receive and retain the fresh falls and drifts of the coming winter.

This particular area of the Central Highlands, where the extensive deer
forests of Mar, Glenfeshie and Rothiemurchus come pretty close to
merging, is one I happen to know through having briefly lived there. The
reason is that during the 1939-45 War I was sent on a mountain and snow
warfare training course. It was based on Glenfeshie (the Feshie being a
tributary of the magnificent Spey) and lasted six weeks, from mid-
November until just before Christmas. Strange to relate, considering that
we could see quite ample traces of former snowfalls in high clefts and
corries like the Braeriach one, we weren't favoured with a single
snowflake throughout the six weeks; and the prevailing weather, though
naturally rather chilly because of the height at which we were living, was
generally drier and pleasanter than one sometimes has to put up with
during an English summer.

Lacking snow, the only ski-ing practice we could get was down dry,
grassy slopes. Similarly, we could learn only in theory the art of building
an igloo or snow-shelter, designed to keep in the heat of a primus stove or
tommy-cooker and keep out bitter winds. But our instructors, led by a
son of Scott the explorer, taught us many a useful tip on how to stay alive
in Arctic cold. Thanks to frequent hill-walking and climbing exploits we

finished the course fitter than ever before. Two experiences in particular I shall never forget.

One was watching from the Lairig Ghru (gloomy pass), on a long, arduous patrol from the Linn o' Dee to Loch Morlich, a golden eagle spreading his great wings no more than a hundred feet above me. No doubt about it, he knows he is the king of birds.

The other lasting memory is of an exercise in which six of us lay along a ridge from which the moorland undulated gently downwards to a fairly wide burn which meandered between irregular banks some 300 yards away. One of our instructors, a sergeant of the Lovat Scouts who had been a stalker before the war, was to cross the burn and mount the slope without being seen or heard. Our task, of course, was to spot him as quickly as we could. I still find it hard to believe, but we saw or heard nothing of Sgt Fraser for the next 40 minutes, and he was within ten yards of us when he stood up in response to a shout from the keenest-eyed member of the group. How he had crossed the burn unsuspected was a mystery, let alone how, wearing camouflaged denims, he had insinuated his tall and hefty person up that stretch of grass and heather as unobtrusively as any snake.

'It was easy enough', he told us, 'because I didn't have to carry a rifle'. Then he added, with a grin, 'But I think I could have picked you off at this range with a pistol'.

So much for reminiscence. Let us resume our journey north via Kincraig, where a unique wildlife park beckons; unique because it

Inveraray, mirrored here in the waters of Loch Fyne (the great sea loch famed for its superlative herring) is a gem of Scottish tourism. Its magnificent castle, still the seat of the Campbells, Dukes of Argyll, is a treasure-house of art and memorabilia; its eighteenth-century courtroom has housed many a famous trial; and one of its churches has a granite bell tower, 126 feet high, which contains Scotland's finest ring of bells.

As this coastal view demonstrates, the sea is the dominant element of life in north-east Fife, known to its inhabitants as the East Neuk (corner). They are justly proud of their ancient maritime royal burghs such as Pittenweem, Crail, Anstruther and St Monans. The first-named, shown here, rises in a series of 'landings', so to speak around its harbour. This form of planning is one of the features which endear its townscape to artists.

accommodates in their natural environment animals and birds such as wolves, bears, wild boar, bison, wild cats, golden eagles and capercailzies, all of which are said to have freely roamed the Highlands in the more or less remote past. The three last-named species can of course still be seen and are believed to be increasing in number. I myself have had a close brush in a wood with a clumsy capercailzie flying jerkily a few feet above the ground and I can readily believe it is the largest game-bird in Britain. And I've already mentioned my lucky view of the eagle.

But I have seen only one wild cat in my life and he, I'm relieved to say, was spitting and snarling in an iron-barred cage at Balmacaan, on Loch Ness-side, some 60 years ago. The wild cat, a creature entirely different from your domestic pussy, is probably the fiercest predator in the British Isles. Largely nocturnal of habit, he will lie up all day in his rocky moorland lair, the sole clue to his presence being the noisome stink of his uncovered droppings. *Pace* the environmentalists, he is in my opinion a native Scotland would be better without.

The stage at which most travellers would be tempted to break their journey north at any season of the year is probably Aviemore. Nowhere I know in Britain has transformed itself so completely. As a youngster I remember the place as little more than a maintenance and operating depot dedicated to the railway. Within the past 20 years or so it has become a major holiday resort, catering for practically every form of sport, recreation and entertainment in or out of doors which a visitor could desire. It has attracted thousands of people, including whole families, who might otherwise never have thought of coming to Speyside. It has also developed into a popular conference centre for businessmen.

Much of the credit for Aviemore's growing prosperity should go to the late Lord Fraser of Allander. It was he, the Glasgow 'master draper' as he liked to style himself, who achieved a life's ambition by acquiring Harrods for his House of Fraser and then, with characteristic initiative and enterprise, turned his attention to promoting Aviemore.

Leaving this object-lesson in how to 'hype' a holiday centre, one may choose between speedily covering the last 30-odd miles to Inverness and taking an attractive Speyside road via Boat of Garten and Dulnain Bridge to delightful Grantown, long recognised as Queen of the Spey Valley. If you aspire to become a connoisseur of Scotch whisky, blended or single (an affinity there to matrimony, because a blend, though based on grain spirit, may often be married, as it were, with malt of diverse origins), there will be no doubt about your choice.

For Grantown-on-Spey, in itself a charming resort, offers easy access by picturesque roads to many celebrated birth-places of famous Highland malts in Morayshire and Banffshire. The very names of the distilleries smack of mountain, loch and glen: like Balmenach, Cragganmore, Dalluaine, Knockando, Dallas Dhu, Benromach, Mannochmore, Glenlossie, Caperdonich, Glen Spey, Craigellachie, Glendullan, Mortlach, Glenfiddich, Cardhu, Balvenie, Benrinnes, Glenallachie and many more.

As for *The* Glenlivet, rightly as proud of its definite article as of its product, one can cite a whole catalogue of other malts linked by hyphen or otherwise to that celebrated designation. For example, Glenburgie, Glenfarclas, Glen Grant, Glen Keith, Glen Moray, Glenrothes, Longmorn,

Smailholm Tower in Roxburghshire, shown here, is probably the best-preserved example of a Border peel tower on public view. Built in the sixteenth century, it is 57 feet high and could still fulfil its purpose, which was to give early warning of the approach of raiders. Easily accessible from Kelso and other towns a few miles away, the tower houses an exhibition of dolls and tapestries on the Border minstrelsy theme.

Miltonduff, Pittyvaich, Strathisla, Tamdhu, Tamnavulin, Aberlour, Tomintoul and Benriach.

The Automobile Association have thoughtfully signposted a 'Whisky Trail' through Speyside which should be a helpful guide for tourists no less interested in the whisky industry — a very important factor in Scotland's economy — than in the scenery. Quite a number of distilleries welcome visitors, subject to advance notice, and some of the managements take upon themselves to maintain the tradition of Highland hospitality. But the wise motorist will leave the 'wee drams' to his passengers.

Like most people who enjoy whisky, I have a favourite malt — which, I confess, comes from a distillery pretty far north of Speyside. But I prefer to relish it in its own exclusive right, sipped neat as an aperitif or from a large, wide-rimmed glass, in lieu of cognac, after a really good dinner. The best selection of single malts I ever tasted was hosted by the late Lord Glenkinglas, a former Secretary of State for Scotland, before and after a dinner he gave for another Scottish journalist, Hugh McMichael, and myself. There were four, and each seemed discernibly different from the others yet equally delicious. As they had been discreetly decanted there was no way of telling the origin, and as guests we forbore to ask.

For regular drinking I would recommend anyone who appreciates Scotch to find by experiment a standard blend of grain and malt which suits his taste — preferably a brand likely to be obtainable wherever he may be — and stay with it. When one's palate has got accustomed to a particular blend, no other can seem quite as satisfying.

It is my impression that in recent years the single malts have become much more popular in England than ever before, thanks partly to skilful marketing which invests them with an aura of fashionable sophistication.

Spirit straight from the still has to be matured in wood, usually oaken casks, for at least three years before it can be legally traded as Scotch whisky. Because they go on improving with maturation, most of the standard blends, but particularly the single malts, remain in the wood for much longer than the minimum requirement. Their stay can be as long as 10 or 12 years.

That is why they are so expensive, not only because of interest on the vast amount of capital thus tied up but because of evaporation — the 'angels' share'. I am told that nearly 20 million gallons of whisky vanish heavenwards over Scotland every year.

A sacrilege I have sadly noticed, in Scottish bars of all places, is the dilution of whisky with lemonade. Large bottles of the stuff stand ready on the counter, to be splashed on request into the customer's glass. When I mentioned this obnoxious trend to a publican, he replied, 'It's the women. More and more of them seem to be switching from gin or vodka and tonic to whisky, but they like to sweeten it a bit. So I have to cater for them — it's my living.' He agreed, however, that it was deplorable to see the generations of tradition, skill, experience and subtle judgement that go into a successful blend wantonly sacrificed in one sugary moment.

Mains water in some big cities may often be scarcely more tolerable than lemonade in whisky. But why put up with it when you can buy a litre of genuine Scottish spring water in the supermarket for thirty pence?

Kelso, seen here from across the splendid river Tweed on which it stands, is not the biggest but one of the most interesting Border towns. It was the site of the largest Border abbey, founded in 1128, which vainly became a fortress against the marauding English in 1545 and was demolished after the garrison, monks included, had been slaughtered. But the tower still stands. The town also has a charming French-style square.

Getting away for the time being from the word and topic which practically stand for Scotland, we can take advantage of the Speyside roads to make for the Moray coast. A diversion to Fochabers would be very much in order, especially about lunch-time, for this thriving little town has a visitor centre which must appeal to everyone with a proper respect for what he eats. It is run by a famous family firm whose perfectly preserved staple foods and delicacies—fruit, vegetables, meats, fish in boundless variety—are prized by eager shoppers everywhere in Britain and in many countries abroad. Their ever-growing success, as any discerning housewife would confirm, is a just reward for their concentration on quality in the product itself and superbly hygienic efficiency in preparing it for the market.

Moray is an ideal home for an enterprise of this kind, because its combination of climate, soil, weather, rivers and sea seems to have been contrived by Providence to produce the best of everything in food and drink. There can be nothing but praise for the local pigmeat, top-grade beef such as you find in London in only the most expensive food halls and luxury hotels, and the ultra-fresh salmon, trout and sea fish. The quality of the vegetables and soft fruit can be compared only with those grown in another favoured area of Scotland, the Carse of Gowrie on Tayside which links Perthshire with Angus.

From Fochabers, granted time to spare, it would be pleasant to head north-east for a look at one or two of the Banffshire fishing villages. Gardenstown, for instance, of which Hardley has provided (p. **86**) an unusual view from the waterside of steep-roofed houses catching the evening sunlight as they cluster together while shadows creep towards them from the rugged heights behind.

But if we were to reach the coast at Cullen, Gardenstown would still be quite a few miles away, well beyond Banff and Macduff. We had better rest content to head westward from Fochabers via Llanbryde to the charming town (city, rather) of Elgin. For me it is always a 'city' because it has the distinction of a beautiful thirteenth-century cathedral, once known as the Lantern of the North. Though savagely put to the flames in 1390 by the Wolf of Badenoch and allowed to fall into ruin after the Reformation, the Lantern of old still retains its luminiscent power to evoke and renew the spirit of a Christian.

From Elgin on the Lossie a few miles will take us to Lossiemouth with its fine golf links and beaches. This was once the holiday home of a Prime Minister, Ramsay Macdonald, and the nearby R.N. air station is nowadays esteemed as the home base of the Air Sea rescue service to whose skill and daring climbers and yachtsmen sometimes owe their lives.

Forres, an increasingly popular resort and residential centre midway between Elgin and Nairn, is graced by some of the most attractive gardens and parkland to be found in Scotland: a tribute to its equable climate as well as to the public-spirited generosity of local boys who made good. On Cluny Hill the Nelson Tower, built in 1806, is an excellent viewpoint from which to find one's bearings in a varied terrain, wooded and hilly to the South and levelling on the seaward side to Findhorn Bay and the Culbin Sands.

That extensive area of fine sand dunes, one of several on Scotland's East

As this view from the sea brings out in the evening light, the Banffshire fishing village of Gardenstown, on its own little bay to the east of Gamrie Head, gives the impression of seeming to hold on very tightly to a steep hill.

Fort George, strategically placed to command the sole seaward access to Inverness Firth, has probably never in its 220 years heard fired in anger the gun shown in this well-chosen study. But it achieved the main purpose of an eighteenth-century fortress, which was, like that of nuclear weapons today, to deter. It has also provided a much appreciated home base for Highland regiments.

Coast, could be seen as a warning to 'let well alone'. Where dune formations have remained stable for a long time they have a fair chance of developing a kind of limey grassland consisting of windblown shell-sand. This marram grass or machair, to adopt the Hebridean term, helps to foster stability and curb the dunes' tendency to shift in response to a stiff onshore wind.

But inhabitants of the Culbin area during the sixteenth and seventeenth centuries would appear to have been foolhardy. Though they must have been told about severe gales which had caused sand to encroach upon good land elsewhere and actually to overwhelm and destroy an Aberdeenshire coastal village, they recklessly persisted in taking marram grass away from the dunes. Nature exacted her condign penalty in 1694, when a night of tremendous storm ended with a large estate east of the Culbin sand-hills completely buried, cottages, farm buildings, growing crops and all, under a thick pall of sand. The lesson was not lost upon the Scottish Parliament in Edinburgh, which passed in 1695 an Act prohibiting the removal of marram from dunes. The Forestry Commission has now skilfully transformed some 7000 acres of desert into woodland.

Let us banish the memory of that sad story by moving on to Nairn, for my money the ideal family holiday resort. With golf courses, tennis courts, swimming pool, safe sandy beach, sailing on Moray Firth, fishing on its own river, it caters unostentatiously for all ages, taste and purses. Above all, the town and the people have about them an air of unhurried relaxation which I find infectious. Perhaps that was part of its attraction for Harold Macmillan when as Prime Minister he went there each summer to play golf on the magnificent championship links.

Nairn's accessibility is a great asset: it has a station on the Aberdeen-Inverness main line, the A9 trunk road to Perth is within easy range, and you can reach Inverness Airport at Dalcross in half-an-hour. I realized the important of the airport facility when, in the hotel bar on my last visit to Nairn, I couldn't help overhearing the conversation of four engineers from nearby Ardersier, in my schooldays a mere village, but now a major oil rig construction centre. They were discussing weekend plans and I was as surprised as were his companions to hear one of them say, in a strong Devon accent, that he would be going home for the weekend 'as usual'.

Not far from Ardersier is Fort George, strategically sited at the end of a short peninsula or tongue of land so as to command the comparatively narrow channel which gives access from the North Sea and Moray Firth to the Inverness Firth. Begun in 1747, the year after Culloden, the Fort took about 20 years to complete. Designed to a perfect geometric plan, it has been considered the finest artillery fortification of its time in Europe, and was so solidly built that it remains much the same today as 200-odd years ago. As may be judged from the state of the brickwork and masonry shown in Hardley's cleverly conceived view from the battlements, (p. **89**) the Army has taken good care of its own.

Having been wounded in action and medically downgraded, I was appointed adjutant at the Fort for the last few months of the 1939-45 War, when it was a Primary Training Centre, and I became quite fond of the old place. Because 1759 happened to be the year of Robert Burns's birth, I loved seeing from my bedroom window each morning that particular

It would be difficult to find a less hackneyed and more vivid view of the much-photographed river Ness than this impression of reflected sunlight at sunset. It's a remarkable little river, flowing only six miles from its source in Loch Ness to its absorption in the Inverness Firth, and seldom more than paddling or wading deep except at flood tide. Yet it is as broad as the Clyde at Jamaica Bridge, Glasgow, and its waters sparkle like any mountain stream's.

date engraved at the top of a rainwater pipe on the wall opposite.

Many years after the War I paid a sentimental visit to the Fort, which by then had become the regimental headquarters of the Queen's Own Highlanders (Seaforth and Cameron). These two grand old regiments, having been merged willy-nilly, had sensibly combined to establish a museum in a building facing the Square. The first item to catch my eye was a portrait of Sir James Cassels, a famous Seaforth officer, under whom I had the good fortune to serve when he commanded, for all too short a posting, our battalion of The Black Watch.

The curator, himself a Seaforth and, by his tongue, a Lewisman, assured me that the Colonel of the Regiment would indeed be visiting the museum soon.

'You must all be very proud of him,' I ventured. 'Ou aye,' was the reply. 'He did pretty well.'

Pretty well! He only became Chief of the General Staff and a Field Marshal.

I thought the meiosis typical of the old-style Highlander, who recoiled from being thought in any way boastful. Such bad form!

With a vast area of Scotland still to cover, it is time we made our way via Croy to Inverness, aptly named the hub as well as the capital of the Highlands. But a halt at Culloden is surely essential, if only to pay our respects to brave men who gave their lives for the vision which they had so confidently espoused at Glenfinnan nine months before.

The last pitched battle on the soil of Great Britain was all over, we are told, in 40 minutes; yet the odds were so overwhelmingly against Prince Charles's 'rebel' force that its losses numbered 1200 (24 per cent of its strength) while the Hanoverian army suffered only 310 (3.44 per cent). The clansmen lie under communal headstones bearing their clan patronymics, the Government soldiers (though not necessarily all English) under a single stone inscribed 'The English were buried here'.

The battlefield is nowadays revered and maintained in a manner worthy of its historic significance. In addition to the memorial cairn, 20 feet high, erected in 1881 there is an informative visitor centre, with audio-visual equipment. Old Leanach farmhouse, the Prince's all too briefly occupied field headquarters, has been restored as a battle museum. And of course the most prominent landmark has always been the massive Cumberland Stone, from which the victorious Duke of Cumberland is said to have viewed and appraised the prospective battlefield early in the day. Once battle was actually joined he was apparently seen in action on his charger immediately behind his front-line troops, exercising personal control of the second echelon.

In contrast to the Prince, the Duke was a trained soldier, well versed in tactical command. From a strictly military point of view, what strikes one as remarkable about Culloden was the comparative youth of both commanders. The Duke had celebrated his 25th birthday only the day before and the Prince was still eight months short of his 26th.

That said, it is not for nothing that Cumberland is still known among some Highlanders with long memories as 'the Butcher'. Whether or not he personally condoned the veritable massacre which followed Culloden, as commander-in-chief he must be held ultimately responsible for the behaviour of his subordinates, and wanton murders such as those committed by a major commanding a troop in Glenmoriston are impossible to forget or forgive.

Coming upon three men innocently engaged in the routine task of harrowing a field, the gallant Major Lockhart promptly shot all three without warning and had their bodies strung up before the laird's eyes. When it turned out that the laird himself had supported the Hanoverian cause his life was spared. But his cattle were driven away, his home was burned down and even his wife's rings and dresses were plundered.

Rather than dwell on such ghastly crimes against humanity—and many are on record—I prefer to remember the fact that the Prince roamed the Highlands unscathed for five months after Culloden with a reward of £30,000 on offer for his capture. Think of the equivalent value today and marvel at the disregard for personal gain which this bespeaks.

Not very far from Culloden is the 'Clootie Well', now styled St Mary's Well but obviously of pre-Christian origin. As youngsters we used to walk there from Inverness on the first Sunday in May, drop in a coin, wish a wish and hang a rag of clothing on a nearby tree.

This view from its frozen shore across Loch Laggan, Inverness-shire, prompts the reflection that a stretch of water high in the Grampians, surrounded by peaks well over 3000 feet, can seldom stay ice-free all winter. When a loch such as this becomes frozen over, the wintering waterfowl are apt to move to lower levels or to the coast.

93

Pines which may be descendants of the Caledonian forest are here reflected in the wintry waters of Loch Lochy, westernmost of the three Great Glen lochs which account for 38 of the Caledonian Canal's 60 miles between Inverness and Corpach, where it enters upper Loch Linnhe. At Banavie, a mile or two north of its terminal point, there is a series of eight locks—known as 'Neptune's Staircase'—which raise the level of the canal by 64 feet.

A mile or two east of the battlefield across the river Nairn are the standing stones and cairns of Clava, an extensive group of megalithic monuments in a remarkable state of preservation though dating from the Bronze Age. There is evidence that they marked some kind of necropolis, but their prehistoric origin and purpose are still in dispute. One theory is that the stone circles were used by primitive man for rituals, perhaps associated with sun-worship, through which he sought supernatural protection against ravening predators and other perils of his time.

Having reached Inverness, I resist the temptation to sing further the praises of my native royal burgh, about which I have already reminisced perhaps more than enough. I would only say that tourists who choose to by-pass the town by making directly for the splendid new Kessock Bridge over the Firth to the Black Isle, Ross and Cromarty, and the far North will deprive themselves of a rich variety of interest and enjoyment.

It can scarcely be doubted that a major factor in the promotion of tourism in the Inverness area during the past half-century has been the world-wide controversy over the existence or otherwise of a Loch Ness 'Monster'. The town, giving easy access to the Caledonian Canal of which the loch in the Great Glen forms part, is a handy base for monster-hunters.

In this connection I have a tale to tell which may be new to many. It concerns the late Dr Evan Macleod Barron, in my opinion the true begetter of the 'Monster' phenomenon. A solicitor and historian as well as editor of the *Inverness Courier*, Barron was a consummate master of what one might call impressionist English, which I take to mean the choice of a particular word to convey to the reader's or listener's mind an image which transcends its everyday meaning.

In May 1933 Alec Campbell, the 'Courier's' district correspondent at Fort Augustus on Loch Ness-side, included in his regular batch of news items a note about reports that some strange large 'beast' or 'creature' had recently been sighted disporting itself on the waters of the loch. Shown by his chief reporter this first-ever mention of such a thing, Barron at once exclaimed, 'If the creature is as big as Campbell says, it's a monster. That's the word to use,' So the chief reporter used it, not only in the 'Courier' but in messages duly telegraphed to daily papers for which he was the accredited correspondent or 'stringer'. This seems to me a perfect example of the fact that one word can make a story. I doubt whether any dispatch about a strange 'beast' or 'creature' would ever have taken Fleet Street's fancy. But the Loch Ness *Monster* has become the longest-running story, war and politics apart, of the twentieth century.

I myself have never seen a trace of it nor even any photograph which I'd accept as convincing evidence that a monster exists. But in 1937 I was assured by a respected Inverness lawyer, an old family friend of absolute integrity buttressed by all the habitual scepticism of his profession, that it does.

Driving homeward one afternoon along the west shore of the loch between Fort Augustus and Invermoriston he had noticed 'a bit of a flurry', as he put it, on the surface of the water about 200 yards out. So he stopped the car and waited: to be rewarded within a few moments by (his words again) 'a clear view of some very large aquatic creature alternately plunging and surfacing, but never showing the whole of its obviously great bulk above the water'.

He watched this performance, he said, for at least 20 minutes. Then, after ten minutes without any further sign of activity, he resumed his journey. His eyesight was good, but of course he had with him neither field-glasses nor camera, let alone another witness. So he had decided to relate his experience only to close friends, for fear of derision. 'And I trust you never to tell it in print,' he added. He being dead long since, this is the first time I have done so.

To use one's own car—with, if possible, a passenger who can share the driving—is probably the most enjoyable way of touring the infinite variety of mountain, loch, river and coastal scenery which lies north and west of the Great Glen. The motorist's advantage consists chiefly in the ability to adapt his planned itinerary to the weather or even to a sudden whim.

But there still exist adequate choice and opportunity for visitors who rely on public transport. Though the contours and sparse population of Wester Ross and Sutherland have combined to make the region unpromising territory for railway engineers, two means of entering by rail the fringes of this gloriously unspoiled natural heritage are available. I have already extolled them both—the West Highland line to Mallaig via Fort William and Highland Rail's westward branch via Dingwall to Kyle of Lochalsh. From certain stations on either of these lines it is possible to connect with bus services or coach tours which penetrate deeply into the interior of the Wester Ross countryside.

Inverness is clearly the best starting-point of all, offering a regular bus service to distant Ullapool on Loch Broom. This must be one of the most scenic bus routes in Britain, running alongside lochs with extensive deer forests and lofty mountains on either hand. Near Braemore, for example, the River Droma, amply charged from its loch, rushes through the deep mile-long Gorge of Corrieshalloch to form the spectacular Falls of Meashach (150 feet), which may be viewed from a suspension footbridge.

During the main tourist season Inverness has a splendid array of all-day coach excursions to Wester Ross destinations as far away as Loch Maree, one of Scotland's finest freshwater lochs, and even Gairloch.

It was from Gairloch while on holiday in September 1921 that the Prime Minister, Lloyd George, called the celebrated Cabinet meeting on the Irish question in the Council Chamber of Inverness. Sadly, the issue remains, apparently perennial, but the holiday habits of Ministers have changed.

Fortunate neighbour of Flowerdale, as beautiful as its name, the charming little resort of Gairloch is on the west coast of a peninsular wedge of land, some five miles wide, which separates the Gair Loch from Loch Maree. That extensive inland loch's waters flow via the short River Ewe into a sea loch of the same name at Poolewe.

The great attraction of this district is the Inverewe sub-tropical garden, where rare and exotic plants and species, not to mention palms, can be seen growing healthily and profusely in the open air—a signal tribute to the equable climate of Ross-shire's Atlantic seaboard, presumably thanks

To capture with a camera this view northwards to Stac Polly from Loch Lurgain, Wester Ross, would entail a venturesome journey, turning left from A835 about 10 miles north of Ullapool. But glorious mountain scenery would make the effort well worthwhile. Though Stac Polly (2009 feet) cannot be called the giant of Inverpolly Forest, its needle ridge is a uniquely tempting incentive for rock climbers.

to the beneficent influence of the Gulf Stream which flows northwards along the west coast. The garden, now operated all year round by the National Trust for Scotland, was created out of bare, rocky ground a century ago by the local laird, Osgood McKenzie, a keen botanist who was also noted in his time for prowess with rod and gun.

Poolewe is inextricably linked in my memory with Ullapool—three sea-lochs away to the north—by a quip with which my father teased us at breakfast more than 60 years ago. 'What is the porridge saying in the pot?' he asked us children. After we had sat for some moments without response he supplied the answer: 'Ullapool, Ullapool, Ullapool, Poolewe, Poolewe, Poolewe.' Strange to say, these place-names, quickly repeated, sound remarkably like the 'plop-plop' of porridge coming to the boil.

One of the sea inlets I have taken the liberty of calling sea-lochs is properly named Gruinard Bay, the others being Little Loch Broom and Loch Broom. Motor-boat trips from Ullapool give access to islands off the deeply indented coast and to the enticing Summer Isles farther north. Ullapool also has a car ferry service plying to Stornoway, Isle of Lewis.

Islands such as Tanera More, Tanera Beg, Horse and Priest (there are fully 25 within reach from Achiltibuie or Ullapool) are no longer inhabited except by birds and animals, nor do they support much vegetation other than grass, heather and bracken. But the Torridonian sandstone of which they were formed by our planet's ancient convulsions gives them a kind of primitive sculptured beauty all their own.

One can imagine nothing more pleasant on a fine clear day than to cruise at ease among the islands, admiring their varied colouring and bird life, then turning one's gaze towards the mainland to enjoy distant views of the high tops in Coigach and beyond, like Ben More Coigach (2438 feet), Cul Beag (2523), Cul Mor (2786) and Stac Polly (2009). As Wester Ross merges with Sutherland there might even be a glimpse or two of Canisp (2779) and the conspicuous Suilven (2399), known from its profile as The Sugar Loaf, which rears its head in Glencanisp Forest, south of Loch Assynt.

The nearest coastal holiday resort is Lochinver, which is also a port for the white fish trade. It is reached from Inchnadamph, at the eastern end of Loch Assynt, by a road which skirts the northern shore of the loch. The whole area between the rivers Inver on the north and Kirkaig on the south, flowing into their namesake sea-lochs, is understandably popular with anglers, for there is 'water, water everywhere'—nearly 300 specific lochs, someone has evidently counted, in the wide-ranging parish of Assynt.

The various heights of the Coigach-Assynt region mentioned above are mostly composed, geologists give us to understand, of a very hard type of Torridonian sandstone, sometimes topped with even harder quartzite, which was laid down by earth movements at least 600 million years ago. It is all very complicated; but for all we know the dramatic beauty of individual 'Torridon Hills' as we see them today may have supplanted some yet more ancient mountain range which was worn away and buried aeons before they ever took shape.

You could make your way towards the glen, river and attractive village of Torridon (which has a deer museum and an audio-visual wild life

An impressive distant view of the rugged heights of the Cuillin Hills in Skye, as seen to the north-west from the cliffs which frown over Loch Scavaig at Elgol on the southern coast of the island. A mountain range in their own right, these spectacular 'hills', mainly well over 3000 feet, are an irresistible challenge to the many climbers they lure to Skye.

display) via Shieldaig, by bus from Strathcarron station on the Kyle line. Shieldaig lies at the head of a sea loch of the same name whose waters unite with those of the very much larger Loch Torridon. The journey through Glen Shieldaig, flanked by cliffs nearly 500 feet high and offering midway a chance to view a splendid waterfall, with lovely woodland and mountain scenery on either side, is an experience in itself.

But Torridon's loch, glen and mountains are even more thrilling. There is no comparable area of the United Kingdom, or perhaps of all Europe, where nature can be observed in more awe-inspiring and ennobling guise. A friend of mine who settled at Torridon after her husband's death told me she owed her relatively contented acceptance of widowhood to the consoling influence of the landscape. 'From the very first morning', she said, 'I realised what the psalmist meant about lifting one's eyes unto the hills. They are the best psychotherapists in the world.' Among the Torridonian hills whence came her aid are Ben Eighe (3309 feet), outstanding for its top of white quartzite rock; Ben Alligin (3232) and Liathach (3456).

For much the same therapeutic reason, a distinguished old soldier in retirement near London considers his summer ill-spent unless it includes two or three weeks at Applecross, a village tucked away on its own little bay some 15 miles across the peninsula from Shieldaig. 'I can sail, I can fish, I can roam Applecross Forest at will,' he says. 'Best of all, I can gaze across the Inner Sound to Raasay and Skye. It renews your faith in the world God made.'

Applecross used to be accessible only by a hair-raising road from Tornapress over the Bealach nam Bo (Cattle Pass). But there is now a coastal road linking the village with Shieldaig and Loch Torridon.

An endearing trait of Ross-shire is the manner in which the whole character of the countryside changes between east and west. Only about 80 miles separate Cromarty, on the Moray Firth, from Gairloch, overlooking the Atlantic, and both are on much the same latitude. Yet the eastern side of the county, generally speaking, rejoices in what one might call a gentle low-key landscape; while the scenic attractions of Wester Ross are its rocky mountains that seem to be reaching for the sky, its great sea-lochs, its towering cliffs and spectacular waterfalls.

If we confine comparison to actual heights, the famous An Teallach (The Forge), a ridge of red sandstone in Strathnasheallag Forest south of Little Loch Broom, rises to 3483 feet, an altitude which Ben Wyvis, the 3429-foot monarch of Easter Ross, comes close to matching. But An Teallach is only one among many 'Munros' (summits above 3000) in Wester Ross, whereas 'the Ben', as it is familiarly known to the people of Inverness, Dingwall and other places within visual range of its singular grandeur, is pretty much in a class by itself.

Easter Ross, however, has many charms of its own which, though they may appeal to the hill-walker, the amateur of Scottish history, the keen golfer and the average family holiday-maker rather than to devotees of mountaineering, geology, sea angling and field sports, ensure its unfailing

No traveller will discover in Scotland, or perhaps anywhere else, views to surpass in thrilling beauty those available from the twin lochs of Shieldaig and Torridon on the west coast of Wester Ross. The Torridon Mountains are an extraordinarily compact range of nine summits, all over 3000 feet, and geologists reckon that the rock of which they are formed could be six or seven hundred million years old.

Smoo Cave, subject of this remarkable picture, is on the far north coast of Sutherland, 1½ miles east of Durness. Breaking into the cliffs by an entrance 53 feet high, which might almost qualify as a man-made Gothic arch, it is in fact the outermost of three vast caverns forming a deep cleft which extends some 150 yards into the limestone rock. The second of these, by no means easy to reach, contains a waterfall. But the third defies access.

popularity. One of its major assets as a holiday centre is that it's comparatively easy to get there and to travel around, by rail as well as by car or bus, once you are there. Touring is easier than ever now that the rather temperamental ferry of old from Inverness to North Kessock, gateway to the Black Isle and points north, has been made redundant by the graceful high-level bridge carrying the Great North Road (A9).

The bridge facility, invaluable though it is, need not dissuade a motorist from steering westward at North Kessock and taking the old road along the north shore of the Beauly Firth via Redcastle and Muir of Ord, there to join A862 for Conon Bridge and then Dingwall, the fine old county seat at the head of the magnificent Cromarty Firth. The charming and dignified little town of Strathpeffer, a late Victorian gem complete with spa and pump-room, is only a four-mile bus ride away.

The Cromarty Firth, one of the world's most secure and spacious naval havens, takes its name from a township of much historic interest at the northern tip of the Black 'Isle' (actually a peninsula). The great firth's narrow entrance is guarded by The Sutors, formidable headlands approaching 500 feet in height, which match coastal cliffs of similar rock a few miles south at Rosemarkie. That favourite resort and its neighbour Fortrose, which share an excellent golf course on Chanonry Ness, whose lighthouse looks across the mouth of Inverness Firth to Fort George, are noted for early Christian antiquities. Chief among these are the beautiful red sandstone remains of Fortrose Cathedral.

Apart from its sixteenth-century parish church, Cromarty's claim to distinction rests on its literary associations. It honours the humble birthplace, a thatched cottage now preserved as a museum, of Hugh Miller (1802-1856), stonemason, geologist, and much esteemed by contemporary writers for his command of English prose. Still admired is his best-known work, *My Schools and Schoolmasters*. Two centuries before Miller, in a castle (long since demolished) overlooking the town, was born Sir Thomas Urquhart, celebrated translator of Rabelais.

Invergordon, on the northern shore of the Firth opposite Cromarty, was during and after the 1914-18 War an extremely important base of the Grand Fleet. In 1931 this convenient and friendly town, well served by road and rail and popular with its sailor guests, incurred undeserved notoriety by chancing to become the venue of the so-called 'Invergordon Mutiny'.

As a callow young reporter I was sent from Dundee to cover this event, but none of us got much closer to it than hanging about the shore canteen where apparently continuous meetings were going on. My main memory is of a distant view across the water of ratings lounging or strolling in most unseamanlike fashion aboard HMS *Hood*, at anchor out in the Firth. I shared with fellow-journalists the impression that the 'mutiny' was no more than an outburst of pent-up resentment against the unfeeling, indeed heartless manner in which Whitehall politicians and bureaucrats had imposed disproportionately severe cuts in pay and allowances upon the ranks least able to bear them.

After a diversionary visit to Invergordon one could choose to follow either A9 or the roughly parallel main railway line northwards in a wide sweep through fine farming country via Tain (shrine of St Duthus) and

Berriedale is a little fishing village at the foot of the cliffs of south-east Caithness, approached from Helmsdale by a famous hill. Quite near is Langwell, the Duke of Portland's estate, where white deer can sometimes be seen.

Very little is left of the ancient Keiss Castle but its tall, slender tower perched on the cliff top on the east coast of Caithness. There is a modern replacement for the castle not far away.

This lovely sunset over Gourock, seen from the monument on Lyle Hill, stretches its colourful mantle over the reach of the Clyde which opens into the Firth considered by many to be the world's greatest yachting expanse. The river's waters mingle hereabouts with those of the Gare Loch and Loch Long.

Morangie (a name I link with heavenly whisky). Alternatively, one could save a dozen miles by choosing the hilly A836 across Strathrory and Allt Dearg to join up with A9 and the railway at Wester Fearn and then follow the southern shore of Dornoch Firth to Ardgay.

The only way to get round the head of the firth, whether by road or rail, is via Ardgay and Bonar Bridge. The railway builders chose to avoid this necessity by forfeiting access to Dornoch, county town of Sutherland and possessor of an early thirteenth-century cathedral restored to public use about 150 years ago.

The town also shares the distinction of the Royal Dornoch Golf Club's championship course. This very old-established facility—its origin can be traced as far back as 1616—is recognized as one of the very finest seaside links in the United Kingdom. Dornoch's attractions can be reached via the north shore of the firth, with a view *en route* of Skibo Castle, which could scarcely be hailed as an architectural showpiece. A vast contemporary structure with no historic associations, it was bought in 1898 by Andrew Carnegie, the Dunfermline-born youngster who made a huge fortune out of steel in the United States and spent much of it endowing free public libraries, scholarships and awards for bravery.

Having detoured inland from Ardgay, the railway crosses Strath Oykel by a viaduct to Invershin, whence it runs northwards alongside the Shin to serve the thriving little market town of Lairg at the southern end of Loch Shin. Lairg is an important centre for sheep markets, and the station, a mile or two out of town, is an extremely useful nexus of communications. It offers bus services to and from such comparatively remote places as Lochinver (47 miles), Laxford Bridge (37), Scourie (44), Durness (56) and Tongue—37 via Altnaharra at the west end of Loch Naver.

A diversion alongside the loch to its other end would take the traveller through the area generally associated with the 'Sutherland clearances' of the early nineteenth century. Evicted in favour of sheep-farming from crofts which were their homes and their living, many blameless Highlanders—the 'displaced persons' of their day—had to seek a future for themselves and their families in the south or abroad. This diaspora helps to account for the remarkable persistence of generations of Scottish ancestry in the 'New World' of the Americas.

One could argue that the landlords' policy for maximizing the commercial return from their unpromising acres has had a beneficial effect on all concerned in the long term. But it has left an ineradicable scar on folk memory. As a boy I was told by an old man that tenantry presented by a Duke of Sutherland with a reproduction of his portrait employed it for a certain sanitary purpose at the bottom of a bucket.

Much of the far north-west interior of the old county of Sutherland, covered with moorland and forest, remains the closest approximation to a barren trackless desert to be found in Great Britain. But there is no doubt that the simultaneous advance of modern roadmaking and the internal combustion engine has opened up its exhilarating scenery of mountain and loch to an extent never known since the days of foot-slogging clansmen. Hydro-electric development, too, though altering the landscape in ways not always appreciated, has played an important part.

A bus ride to Kinlochbervie on the west coast, or to the Kyle of

Durness on the north, could take you within range of wild Cape Wrath and its lighthouse. Durness is only a mile or so from the phenomenal and awe-inspiring Smoo Caves pictured here.

Near Kylesku, where a free ferry for walkers is approachable by a road running northwards from Loch Assynt, you could make your way on foot to the highest waterfall in the British Isles. Its name is Eas a Chual Aluinn. Not far from Loch Glencoul, the fall measures 658 feet. So it not only dwarfs the better known and much acclaimed Falls of Glomach in Wester Ross but is four times higher than Niagara itself.

Having penetrated far into Sutherland with our excursions from Lairg station, let us assume that our journey's end, in accordance with convention, is John o' Groats in Caithness. So we can return to the east coast by road (A839) or rail via Strath Fleet and The Mound, where the Highland line and A9 resume their roughly parallel course. Their route north runs by way of Golspie and then Brora, model little Highland towns.

Golspie is noted for its proximity to Dunrobin Castle, the famous and formidable, almost ostentatious 'stately home' which has been for centuries the seat of Earls and Dukes of Sutherland. There is also an oversized statue of the 1st Duke atop the summit of noble Beinn a Bhragie a mile or two inland. What an outsize inferiority complex is there revealed! In my view Golspie better deserves to be noted, judging by former pupils I have met, for the quality of its schools than for its ducal associations.

Brora's claim to fame, apart from its excellent salmon river and other sporting amenities, is its unique little coal mine, a geological curiosity which is still in continuous production after about 400 years. Hugging the coast as far as Helmsdale, another salmon fisherman's delight, the railway veers inland again up the Strath of Kildonan—where there was a mini-gold rush in 1896—and makes its gloriously scenic way from Sutherland into Caithness by romantic-sounding places such as Kinbrace, Auchentoul Forest, Forsinard and Altnabreac to Georgemas Junction. Here the line divides, one track turning south-east for Wick, the other setting a course north for the terminus at Thurso.

If travelling by road, you will have remained faithful to A9 all the way up the coast to Latheron, where the choice lies between A895 going due north for Thurso, and continuing coastwise with A9 for Wick and, ultimately, John o' Groats.

I confess to being no great enthusiast for the last-named destination, which has struck me as being one of those places where it is more important and rewarding to be able to say you have been than actually to be. It has the merit, if such there be, of finding itself 876 miles from the British mainland's other diagonal extremity, Land's End, and of course it commands impressive views across the stormy Pentland Firth to Stroma and Orkney. But those who believe it to be Britain's most northerly point, barring islands, deceive themselves. That distinction belongs to Dunnet Head, which can be reached from a junction at Dunnet about halfway along the north coast road to Thurso.

Just north of this road is the Queen Mother's favourite retreat, the Castle of Mey, with the lovely gardens she has created. I would estimate that when in residence there the dear lady is just about as far north as those

OVERLEAF

The Abbey Church of Paisley, shown here in a colourful springtime setting, has triumphed over many vicissitudes to remain a glory of Scottish ecclesiology. Founded in 1163, it was almost destroyed by Edward I in 1307, only to begin rising again after Bruce's victory at Bannockburn. But in 1553 the tower collapsed, wrecking much of the structure below, and for 350 years only the nave was useable for worship. To the great credit of 'Paisley buddies', 30 years' restoration was completed in 1928.

G reenock in Renfrewshire is no
longer the major shipbuilding
and industrial town it was a few
years ago and one doesn't see many
ocean liners waiting in the Clyde
roadstead by the 'Tail o' the Bank'.
But the busy scene in its Victoria
Harbour, pictured here, indicates
that there could well be better times
ahead for a skilled and enterprising
workforce.

who have striven to reach John o' Groats.

Wick and Thurso are pleasant and interesting towns which would well repay at least an overnight stay. Wick, with a population of about 8000, a good harbour, an airport close at hand, and rail and bus services to the south, is the administrative centre for Caithness and is reckoned the most important town north of Inverness. It has ample sporting and recreational facilities. It is also within easy reach of some spectacular rock scenery and fine old castles, including Freswick, on the A9 north of the town, which has remains of Viking homesteads nearby.

The population of Thurso, 21 miles north-west of Wick on its namesake river and bay (the derivation is Norse, meaning 'Thor's stream') has grown three-fold since the Atomic Energy Authority's development station for fast reactors producing electrical power was established at Dounreay. Thurso's population now exceeds 9000 and the atomic power station, on the edge of the coast, about eight miles west of the town, is a great attraction for townspeople and tourists. Visitors are made welcome at a free exhibition which is open from May to September.

From Scrabster Harbour, two miles north of Thurso along the west shore of the bay, there are daily steamers to and from the Orkney Isles. Thurso's chief historical relic is its ruined castle, birthplace and family seat of Sir John Sinclair (1754-1835), who compiled the celebrated 'Statistical Account' of Scotland.

As a young reporter covering the final stage of Lloyd George's Land's End to John o' Groats campaign in 1929, I had the pleasure of being shown over what was left of Thurso Castle by his descendant Sir Archibald Sinclair (later the first Viscount Thurso). I still remember 'Archie Sinclair' as the handsomest and most courteous politician I ever knew.

You won't find a wealth of trees in Caithness, nor indeed mile after mile of wooden fence posts, for the fields are usually bounded by Caithness flagstones standing on end—the same hardwearing Castletown stone as used to be shipped in large quantities from Thurso or Wick to form the pavements of great cities in the south. What you surely will experience in this remotest north-west outpost of Britain's mainland is the thrill of wide rolling landscapes—yes, and seascapes too—which imbue the spirit with an exhilarating sense of untrammeled, spacious freedom. If you want the kind of holiday that clears away cobwebs, Caithness is the place for you.

In the civil courts 'discovery' is taken to mean the compulsory disclosure by one side or the other of relevant documents. It therefore seemed proper, in writing about the discovery of Scotland, to concentrate upon the scenic beauty which is generally held to be the country's most relevant attraction.

I confess, rather belatedly, that in doing so I have been unfair to three of Scotland's four major cities—'counties of cities', as they used to be known before the latest shake-up of local government. Justice has been done, I trust, to Aberdeen; but scant attention has so far been paid to the

merits of Glasgow, Edinburgh or Dundee.

Edinburgh is so famous the world over as Scotland's capital that its councillors and residents seem content to take their city's precedence for granted. No wonder. Oft-repeated traditional compliments like 'the modern Athens'; 'mine own romantic town'; 'the finest street in Europe' (Princes Street) and so on could hardly have failed to endow them with an impermeable 'guid conceit o' themselves' and their city.

Perhaps the time has come to warn them, in case they hadn't noticed, that Glasgow has in recent years come up very strongly in public esteem. Of course this upward trend was given a tremendous boost by the inauguration in October 1983 of the purpose-built Burrell Gallery at Pollok Park and its unique one-man collection, which gained instantly favourable publicity throughout the United Kingdom followed by international acclaim. For instance, a professional friend of mine from Buckinghamshire spent three holidays in Glasgow during the Burrell's first year and intends to spend many more because Glasgow itself has taken his fancy.

The re-appraisal of Glasgow as a place to visit—and, more important, a place that wanted and liked to be visited—really began with a communal decision to cleanse its magnificent central buildings of the dirt, soot and grime that had shrouded them for many decades.

Glasgow had earned few compliments from visitors since Daniel Defoe called it in 1723 'the beautifullest little city' he had ever seen. But the urge to prove itself once again worthy of St Mungo and the early-Gothic Cathedral built on the site of his cell kindled such public and private enthusiasm that the late Poet Laureate, Sir John Betjeman, felt justified in hailing Glasgow as the finest specimen of Victorian architecture in Europe.

The reason why Glasgow's nineteenth-century industrial and commercial entrepreneurs could choose to conduct their business from those palatial edifices in the city centre and then be driven home in their broughams to elegant terraces and crescents in the west end was, of course, that they made a great deal of money. Taxation was light, sterling stood high, wages were low—probably much too low.

But some of those wealthy men were not without their own variety of civic conscience, which expressed itself in a form of patronage that is still conferring cultural benefit on the whole community several generations later. They befriended and encouraged talented Scottish artists and were guided by the standards thus set in becoming discriminating art collectors. Old Masters and contemporary paintings acquired for their own homes were in due course presented or bequeathed, like Sir William Burrell's in 1944, to their fellow-citizens as a whole.

Glasgow's great municipal collections are only one of the reasons for regarding it as Scotland's self-financing capital of the arts. It is also the home base of the Scottish National Orchestra, Scottish Opera and Scottish Ballet, all of which are welcome wherever they perform; and it possesses Scotland's only opera house, the Theatre Royal.

Edinburgh, too, has ample centres of culture. But it is hard to think of many, apart from the splendid Usher concert hall, which do not owe their continued existence to the bounty of the national taxpayer. The city

This beautiful vista of sunset over the Scottish capital was photographed from Calton Hill, an urban eminence on which, like McCaig's Tower at Oban, there was intended to be a reproduction of the Parthenon. Begun in 1824 to commemorate Scots killed in the Napoleonic wars, the project had to be abandoned, conspicuously incomplete, for lack of funds. There was already on Calton Hill a Nelson Monument 102 feet tall.

derives substantial cash flow from being the administrative headquarters of Government in Scotland and from its traditional dominance in the lucrative spheres of law, banking, insurance and finance. Yet home-grown benefactors seem pretty thin on the ground, to judge from the annual struggle to fund the city's outstanding post-war artistic achievement, the International Festival of music and drama.

When all is said, however, Edinburgh's severest critic would have to admit that its Castle, Rock, Royal Mile, Palace of Holyroodhouse, Mound, Parliament House, Princes Street Gardens, High Kirk of St Giles, Calton Hill (from which the photograph on p. **118** was taken), Arthur's Seat, Scott Monument, Botanic Gardens, imaginatively sited Zoo and perfect Georgian New Town all contrive to make it 'look the part' as no surrogate capital could. And one could forgive the City Fathers almost anything for having provided at Meadowbank Stadium a convenient arena for the Commonwealth Games.

Having earned my living in Dundee, Glasgow and Edinburgh, I can truthfully say that I enjoyed them all: Edinburgh most of all, perhaps, because I looked forward to a lifetime exploring its endlessly fascinating historic associations. Nowhere else I know, even the Palace of Westminster or the Tower of London, evokes the past so vividly.

All three Scottish cities—and also Aberdeen, as I have earlier tried to show—share the advantage of quick and easy access to the surrounding countryside. From Glasgow you can be off to the Campsie Hills or a choice of country parks; from Edinburgh to the Pentlands or Colinton.

Dundee citizens are perhaps best served of all, with their own sandy beach at Broughty Ferry, the extensive Caird and Camperdown parks within the city boundary, and the rugged Sidlaw Hills and fertile Carse of Gowrie just beyond. The glens of Angus and Perthshire are only a cycle or bus ride away and the Tay road bridge has opened up the Fife side of the Firth.

Even in its hey-day of 'jute, jam and journalism' Dundee presented a startling contrast between great wealth and near-privation. Since then it has had more 'downs' than 'ups' industrially and has had to yield to Aberdeen its rank as Scotland's third city in terms of population. But it has bred a cheerful, self-reliant, adaptable people quite capable of shaping their city's future.

Dundee's situation, rising from the northern foreshore of the Tay estuary as Lisbon rises from the Tagus, seems to engender a hopeful outlook every morning. This is well expressed, I used to think, in the name of one of its oldest humble streets—'Peep o' Day Lane'.

A Gaelic Glossary

Gaelic is probably as often an acquired skill as a mother tongue in Scotland today. Even in the Hebrides and on the west coast, in communities where the language may still be in everyday usage, it would be rare to encounter anyone but a very old inhabitant who did not also 'have the English'. So there should seldom be any difficulty in making oneself understood.

But when planning an itinerary or checking one's position on the ground against place-names on a large-scale map it might be quite helpful to know the meaning of certain words of Celtic (or perhaps Pictish) origin which have a topographical connotation.

Here is a random selection:

Aban	*Backwater.*
Aber	*Mouth of a river; confluence of streams.*
Ach	*Field.*
Allt (ault, alt)	*Burn, stream.*
Ard	*Headland.*
Bal	*Place; farm.*
Ban (bain)	*White; fair-haired.*
Bealach	*Pass, defile, gorge.*
Bearnach	*Gap, cleft, narrow pass.*
Beg (beag)	*Small, short.*
Beithi	*Birch tree.*
Ben (beinn, beann)	*Mountain, high place.*
Bruach	*Brae, slope, bank.*
Bught	*Sheep fold.*
Cairn	*Heap or mound of stones.*
Caisteal	*Castle.*
Calltain (calltuin)	*Hazel tree.*
Cam	*Crooked, distorted, blind in one eye.*
Capull	*Horse, mare, colt.*
Ceardaich	*Smithy, forge.*
Chreagan	*Rocky.*
Clach	*Stone.*
Cnoc	*Hillock, knoll.*
Corrie	*Mountain glen.*
Coul	*Hidden place.*
Creag	*Stone, rock.*

Dail	*Meeting; level ground.*
Darach	*Oak tree.*
Dearg	*Red, ruddy, red-hot; red deer.*
Dobhair	*Water; Border (of territory).*
Droma (druim)	*Ridge of a hill.*
Druman	*Ridge; roof; elder tree.*
Dubh (duibhe)	*Dark, black; sad.*
Dun	*Fortress; tower; castle.*
Easbuig	*Bishop.*
Ess (eas)	*Waterfall; cataract; stream with steep, high banks.*
Eun	*Eagle (the bird); bird; fowl.*
Gall	*Stranger; foreigner; Scotsman who cannot speak Gaelic.*
Gask (gasgan)	*Long strip of land tapering to a point.*
Glas	*Grey, pale, wan, sallow.*
Gorm	*Blue; green.*
Inch (insh)	*Island in river: meadow, piece of arable land.*
Inver	*Mouth of a river.*
Kil	*Church; grave.*
Kin	*Head, chief, top.*
Kyl	*Wood, forest.*
Leamhan	*Elm tree.*
Loch	*Lake.*
Lochan	*Small lake, pond, pool.*
Mam	*Large round hill with no peak.*
Meal	*Large mass, big shapeless hill; mound.*
Merk	*Measure of land.*
More (mhor)	*Large.*
Raich	*Antlers.*
Rath	*Strongpoint; defended place; residence.*
Ruadh	*Reddish; red deer; hind; roe.*
Slochd	*A hollow; basin.*
Sron	*Promontory; nose; prow.*
Struathan	*Streams; currents.*
Talchan	*Low-lying, flat land.*
Tom (tuim)	*Round knoll, hillock, any round heap.*
Tor (tur)	*Tower; fortification; castle.*

Church of the Holyrood, Stirling. The building dates from 1414. It was here that John Knox preached the sermon at the coronation of the 13-month-old James VI in 1567.

Note: The English equivalents given above, being variable, cannot be taken as accurate in every case.

   Some of the Gaelic 'words' listed usually occur as prefixes.

Jedburgh Abbey seen from Jed Water, Roxburghshire. The Abbey, founded in 1118 by David I, was restored to its present condition by the ninth Marquess of Lothian.

124

L och Awe, its calm waters
adorned in this attractive study
by a beautiful sunset, lies at the very
heart of Argyllshire. It is Scotland's
longest freshwater loch, just over 25
miles from end to end, and is
naturally a great favourite with
anglers. A feature is the fifteenth-
century Kilchurn Castle, once the
family seat of the Breadalbanes, on a
little island near the northern head of
the loch.